ENDURING
TRADITIONS

Art of the Navajo

ENDURING TRADITIONS

Art of the Navajo

PHOTOGRAPHS BY *Jerry Jacka*

WRITTEN BY *Lois Essary Jacka*

INTRODUCTION BY *Barton Wright*

NORTHLAND PUBLISHING

First Edition 1994
ISBN 0-87358-584-4
Library of Congress Catalog Card Number 94-25488

Cataloging-in-Publication Data

Jacka, Lois Essary.
    Enduring traditions : art of the Navajo / text by Lois Essary Jacka ; photographs by Jerry Jacka ; introduction by Barton Wright. — 1st ed.
        p.   cm.
    Includes bibliographical references and index.
    ISBN 0-87358-584-4 : $55.00
    1. Navajo art. 2. Navajo artists. I. Jacka, Jerry D. II. Title.
    E99.N3J25 1994
    704'.03972—dc20   94-25488

The text type was set in Granjon and Perpetua
The display type was set in Trajan
Composed in the United States of America
Manufactured in Hong Kong by Toppan
Designed by Trina Stahl
Edited by Susan Tasaki and Erin Murphy
Production Supervised by Lisa Brownfield

0490/10M/8-94

COVER: Solitary Deity, *Detail of a 50" by 40" oil and mixed media on canvas by Tony Abeyta. A mixture of sand and acrylic polymer was used to create the sculptural quality.*

ENDSHEETS: *Miniature Navajo rugs in a variety of styles ranging in size from 2 1/2" by 3 1/2" to 3 1/2" by 5".*

HALF TITLE: Her Beauty Reflects Her Soul, *50" tall bronze by Larry L. Yazzie.*

FRONTISPIECE: Spirits of the Last Light Steamboat, *a 60" by 40" acrylic on canvas by Baje Whitethorne Sr. Baje says that the sky "represents the generations who have gone on—the spirits of the past." In the foreground are two yei'iis who go to each hogan to gather food during certain winter ceremonies.*

THIS PAGE: *Eighteenth century Navajo rock art, northwestern New Mexico*

OPPOSITE: *These wood carvings, part of a set of sixteen participants in the Nightway ceremony by Tom W. Yazzie, won First Prize at the 1967 Gallup Intertribal Indian Ceremonial. From left: a woman holds a basket filled with cornmeal; the medicine man or hataali; Talking God; and Water Sprinkler (who acts the clown and usually appears at the end of the line). The next three figures with square masks are female yei'iis; the last three are male.*

CONTENTS

Stories Our Grandfather Told Us, *a 26" by 19" watercolor by Harrison Begay (Haskey Yahne Yah). Visions of the Holy People fill the minds of children sitting spellbound as they listen to Grandfather's stories.*

PREFACE

Navajo, art. The two are inseparable. Expressing beauty has long been a part of the Diné *lifestyle and the tradition is not just continuing, it is advancing with giant strides.*

That is why we chose to embark on a project that would totally consume our lives for more than a year. Due to the number of talented Navajos who are creating beautiful art objects, we knew we would have an abundance of exceptional art from which to choose. However, selecting from that "abundance of exceptional art" is exactly what caused the most headaches and heartburn—and heartache. Literally dozens of deserving artists had to be omitted due to lack of space.

In selecting art for this book, we relied on the expertise of museum and gallery personnel, traders, judges of Native American art exhibitions, and even artists recommending other artists. We have made every effort to feature the very best of Navajo art. Now we simply place it on stage for, you, the audience to judge for yourself.

We hope this glimpse into the *Diné* culture and the lives of the artists will give you an added appreciation for both, as well as for Navajo art. We present more of the "why" of their art than the "how," as artists share their traditions, legends, history, personal stories, and insights.

We greatly appreciate the time spent with each of them and their openness and willingness to share even intimate details of their lives.

This book is dedicated to the *Diné,* artists and non-artists alike. To all of our Navajo friends and to each and every artist, we can only say *Ahéhee'*—May you always walk the Pollen Pathway.

Jerry and Lois Jacka

INTRODUCTION

ABOVE: *This 12" by 9" watercolor entitled* Woman at Shiprock *was painted by Gerald Naylor in 1936. Naylor was one of the noted easel artists of that time.*

OPPOSITE: *The roots of Navajo art are found in the eighteenth century rock art of* Dinétah, *the legendary Place of Emergence and ancestoral homeland of the Navajo in northwestern New Mexico. The series of petroglyphs shown here may well have been the work of a* hataałi *recording a song or chant for posterity. According to the almost—ninety-year-old* hataałi *Carl Taylor, these symbols resemble one of his horse songs. With daughter Anita Gene translating, Carl explained that songs are sung to keep the horses in harmony. "If you sing to them," he said, "You will have a good horse. If your horse wanders off, you can sing to him and he will return. The songs can also be used in ceremonies." Carl interpreted the Navajo petroglyph panel as follows, from left to right: zigzag lines with arrows represent the Male Rain and lightning coming from the terraced design, a cloud symbol. The horned figure is* Johonaa'ei, *the Sun. At the bottom of the panel is a geometric figure symbolizing Mother Earth, a small horse, and another lightning design that streaks across the panel to a second horse. Above Mother Earth is a deer followed by a horse; two figures representing the Hero Twins of Navajo legend, Monster Slayer and Born for Water; a small deer (below); a second terraced cloud symbol; and a criss-crossed diamond, a symbol for the largest star or possibly the Milky Way. The last design represents lightning and hail, a big wind—a tornado. "That's the way we read them when I was a little boy," Carl said.*

PREVIOUS PAGE: *An eighteenth-century Navajo petroglyph. The deity Ghaa ask'idii (the Humpback Yei'ii) faces a series of five rings. Above his head is a handprint. Moccasin tracks appear to the right of his legs. He is surrounded by an array of animal tracks and an hourglass figure, the symbol for Born for Water, one of the Hero Twin sons of Changing Woman.*

INTRODUCTION

BY BARTON WRIGHT

All mankind shares a propensity for art, and this propensity manifests itself in many forms.

It is a honing of perceptions, of feelings, relationships, and actions.

It is the human imagination unfettered, the stuff of dreams given reality,

and the range of its expressions is limitless.

It matters not whether the outpouring of expression is lavished on sand or pounded plant residue, cliff walls or highway overpasses, the results carry social or religious content. They are renderings meaningful within the group, although they are usually the merest indication of the cultural values they represent. It is the depth of those beliefs that establishes and holds a tradition that can span the centuries, and this is what sustains the artistic tradition of the Navajo.

This tradition itself developed from a fusion of Pueblo, Spanish, and Navajo styles and materials. Pueblo ways came forcefully to the Navajo in the seventeenth century, as, in the ferocious aftermath of the Pueblo Revolt of 1680, large numbers of Pueblo people from the Rio Grande fled northward into the

3

maze of canyons along the upper San Juan River to join the nomadic hunters of north-central New Mexico. Here in the *Dinétah,* the ancestral homeland of the Navajo, is where our first glimpses of these interesting people occur. As the Pueblo refugees flooded in among these indigenous hunters, they brought with them their cultural baggage, things previously unknown to the *Diné,* as the Navajo are more properly called.

Along with these Pueblo people came the prosaic practices of growing corn, erecting masonry houses, and weaving blankets, as well as the dictates of their complex religious and social systems. The *Diné,* on the other hand, brought to the equation an openness to change and the ability to adapt most innovations to their own needs. During the decades of mingling of the two peoples, intermarriage was a common occurrence, and it furthered the infusion of cultural change. If, as it is frequently said, adaptation is the key to survival, then the people of the *Dinétah* could look forward to a bright future.

A scanty but tantalizing record of that mingling of people and the exchange of lifeways remains in the *Dinétah.* There are strange buildings on the mesa tops and spires of rock, while more profuse on the canyon walls are symbols of religious icons, legendary beings, and enigmatic emblems of both Pueblo

This unusual 51" by 31" weaving of Germantown yarn was made around 1890 and is an example of three early Navajo weaving innovations: multiple rug patterns, pictorial elements, and three versions of the "Tree of Life" design.

and *Diné.* Alternating and intermingling on the hundreds of rock surfaces, carefully pecked into the cliff faces, or painted under protective overhanging walls, these signs are as interleaved as were the people who made them. It is here in the remote *Dinétah* that the first glimmerings of a unique artistic tradition are found, one that continued to develop through the next two-and-a-half centuries.

Weaving is one of the earliest indications of the vigorous nature of this interchange and the tradition that developed from it. Because cotton requires a specific ecological niche in which to grow, it remained an item of scarcity for weaving. The acquisition of sheep, however, introduced a steady supply of fiber, a prerequisite to intensive weaving. Why weaving shifted from being a male occupation among the Pueblo to a female industry among the Athapascans (a grouping of Indians that includes the Navajo) is moot, but still an important event. Once it occurred the die was cast, for not only did the women master weaving, but once they began, they wove prodigiously! In the hundred years after the Pueblo Revolt of 1680, Spanish chroniclers noted their work with progressively more emphasis. Croix, in 1780, barely mentions that the Navajo were weavers, but fifteen years later, Chacon declares that their weavings surpassed those of the Spaniards in "delicacy and taste." Within another five years, their weaving was sufficient for their own needs, and they were beginning to trade with others. By 1812, only ten years after this, Pino noted that in the three large northern provinces, the Navajo led all others, even the Pueblo, in the making of woolen fabrics.

Early examples of Navajo jewelry. The three conchos are from a belt made around 1870; the squash blossom necklace belonged to Hoskininnii, a well-known Navajo leader in the Monument Valley area, and dates from the 1880s; the sectioned belt buckle (right) was made from silver-plated Santa Fe Railway brakemen's badges around 1920–30; the brass bracelet, one of the earlier examples of Navajo metal jewelry, was made prior to 1870.

Unfortunately, there are few examples remaining from this early period; whether they were unrecognized or were simply worn out is unknown. From the fragments that have survived, it is obvious that Navajo women had learned to make the basic patterns of stripes, bands, ticking, stepping, and simple diamonds, and were able to produce them in very fine weaves. Building rapidly on this foundation, each successive generation of weavers has experimented and expanded upon the work of its predecessors. Although there have been times when outside influences, the whims of traders, markets, and the like, have had an impact upon Navajo weaving to its detriment, in general, the trend has been toward more individual and greater artistic efforts. Recognition of the artistic merit as well as technical excellence have combined to produce the finest weaving yet achieved by Navajo women, and the tradition continues to develop.

Silver working, one of the other most notable traditions among the Navajo, has a more complex history. Although it is generally accepted that the first

RIGHT: *Navajo bow guards or ketohs of*
silver with leather arm bands. The three
stamped pieces at the left were made during
the late 1800s; the two cast pieces with
turquoise settings are from the 1930s; the
cast piece at lower right dates between 1900
and 1915.

BELOW: *This early pitch-covered coiled*
basketry water bottle, 11 3/4" tall, was
purchased from a Navajo at the 1896
World's Fair in Chicago.

Navajo smith, Atsidi Sani, learned the craft of metalworking from a Mexican
blacksmith named Cassilio sometime around1853, this does not mark the beginning of the use of silver by the *Diné*. Instead, it indicates the point at which
Navajo production of silver work began. Evidence of their fondness for and use
of silver may be found in many early documents that describe the attire of the
Navajo. An example is a letter in 1795 from Governor Fernando de Chacon to
the military commander of Chihuahua, remarking not only on the quality of
Navajo weaving but on the fact that "the Navajo captains are rarely seen without
silver jewelry ." Other records indicate that it was customary for the *Diné* to
adorn not only themselves and their clothing with silver, but their horses and
their riding gear as well. The men's costume, patterned after that of the Spanish,
easily lent itself to embellishment with buttons along the openings of split-legged
pantaloons, and concho belts to hold both shirt and pants. Earrings, bracelets, and
necklaces adorned their bodies. With the attachment of silver ornaments, the
ketoh, the wrist-protector of the archer undoubtedly decorated long before silver
was acquired, became the ultimate expression of men's jewelry. Medicine bags
and tobacco flasks were decorated in similar fashion. Decoration of the women's
costume lagged behind that of the men until the old poncho-style dress was
replaced during Bosque Redondo times by the Mother Hubbards favored by the
American women of that era. These long, flowing garments were easier to decorate and soon were awash in silver buttons, collar edgings, and concho belts.

When the Navajo acquired horses from the Spanish, they took not only the
animals but the riding gear as well, with its remnants of European armor and
equestrian elegance. Bridles boasted chin straps with rows of tinklers, silver

ABOVE: *Navajo pottery of the 1920s. These two Dinnebito polychrome vessels are characteristic of Navajo pottery that was strongly influenced by the Hopis. The bowl at left is 9" in diameter and 4 3/4" deep; the one at right is 6 3/4" in diameter and 3 1/2" deep.*

RIGHT: *Navajo pottery. Left: vessel from Cow Springs, an imitation of the white man's coffee pot, 8" tall, circa 1929. Center: pot (inverted) with two banded designs below the rim, 11 1/2" tall, nineteenth century. Right: Dinétah gray pot, 17 1/2" tall, probably eighteenth century.*

conchos overlapped joints, sheets of embossed silver were wrapped about all the leather straps, and eventually even the saddles sported silver appurtenances.

In the period prior to 1850, acquisition of silver ornamentation came either by direct trade with the Spanish and the Plains Indians, frequently ignored by cultural historians, or by raids that looted the holdings of the inhabitants of pueblos and other outlying communities. During this interval, contact between those who made silver ornaments and those who desired the ornaments was insufficient to allow the transfer of metalworking craft, particularly since the parties in question were more often at war than at peace. For the novice to learn from the craftsman, there must be not only time but tools and raw materials. Thus, it was the mid-nineteenth century before conditions were such that the Navajo Atsidi Sani could learn blacksmithing and apply that knowledge to the making of silver ornaments, thereby becoming the "father" of Navajo silverwork and the initiator of distinctive tradition.

Not all of the crafts that the Navajo are noted for today were derived from outside sources. Some have continued unchanged, while others have been adapted or their function changed. Two of these were basketry and pottery, which the Navajo possessed when they were first encountered, and which have survived into contemporary times. The continuation of a craft item is always dependent upon the need of the culture in which it exists, but frequently, that need becomes subverted through the course of time, and its function may become completely different. The ceremonies of the Navajo required large, flat baskets. The making of these became surrounded by ever-greater ritual proscriptions as time passed— so many, in fact, that their production was virtually prevented. To overcome this problem, the Navajo traded with their neighbors, the Ute and the Paiute, who could make these baskets with the proper patterns but without the hindrance or expense of the necessary ritual. Consequently, one of the best-known Navajo basket designs, the so-called wedding basket, is not made by Navajo at all, although the pattern is dictated by them. Their use of it is unchanged and it remains an integral part of their culture. The pattern, however, has now become a staple and is used not only by the Ute and Paiute, but by the Havasupai and the Hopi as well, for purposes of their own. On the other hand, the production of the Navajo

ABOVE: *Early Navajo baskets ranging in diameter from 11 1/2" to 14". The basket at the top, a classic example of the wedding basket, dates to the 1890s, the other two from the early 1900s. The designs on the one at right are sometimes referred to as Spider Woman Crosses.*

BELOW: *A shallow cave in northwestern New Mexico protects these eighteenth-century Navajo pictographs from the elements. They are believed to be representations of Holy People. The figure at the left may be* Ghaa ask'idii *(the humpback* yei'ii) *and the next one, which has a triangular headpiece, may be Fringe Mouth.*

Wild Mustangs, *a 13 1/2" by 22"*
watercolor, was painted by Quincy
Tahoma in 1956.

utilitarian water bottle, pitched with piñon gum, was not ritually controlled, and the women have never stopped making them. However, with the acquisition of other kinds of containers from the outside world, their purpose changed; now, the water bottles are still made by Navajo women, but as a craft item rather than a necessity.

The original Navajo pottery, simple and elegant in form, has shifted through time to less useful forms. The early elongated vases with pointed bottoms were admirably suited for being slightly embedded in the soil, where they maintained their stability. Simple fillets of clay confined to the visible portion of the rim were the only decoration. As metal containers were acquired from the white traders and settlers, the use of native pottery languished, and the early shapes were often replaced with imitations of coffee pots or cups, stew bowls, or other aberrations. Near the Hopi Reservation, interaction between the two cultures produced an amalgam of shapes resembling first Hopi, then Navajo, with decorations decidedly those of Third Mesa Hopi, but in time these efforts faded. By the mid-twentieth century, just when it seemed that Navajo pottery would disappear, a resurgence began, but not of the old forms. Instead, fat-bodied jars with acorns and oak leaves and other motifs strange to the Navajo appeared. Yet a market developed and the pottery slowly began to acquire greater sophistication, with polished surfaces or fine glazes of piñon gum. Some Navajo, both men and women, took inspiration from the pottery of the Rio Grande and began to produce beautiful polychrome vessels, often with incised decoration. Thus, the

Navajo jewelry of the early 1900s. The earliest Navajo jewelry did not include stonework, but by the 1920s and '30s the use of turquoise had become popular, ultimately resulting in massive rows and clusters of stones that dominated the silverwork.

craft of pottery-making has not been lost for the Navajo, but the tradition of form has almost completely disappeared.

Although the artistic expression of the *Diné* assuredly found outlet in the simple elegance of their crafts, it was primarily in the beauty and intricacies of their sandpaintings, the poetry of their chants, and the symbolism of their mythology that it reached its greatest development. There are no limits to the constructions of the mind, but there are limitations in the use of sand or rock surfaces for the execution of visual representations of those perceived concepts. To make manifest in colored sand the beings that peopled their mythology, and to incorporate these into the many rituals that afforded protection, offered cures, and reordered the world, was an achievement of note. For the artists to produce their rich imagery in such an unforgiving media required a paring-down, a reduction of content to a symbolic shorthand, a process apparent in other examples of their flat art.

It was probably inevitable that a desire to preserve the evanescent beauty of the sandpainting, always destroyed at the end of the day that it was made, would lead to methods of recording it. It was early in the twentieth century that Dr. Kenneth Chapman discovered a Navajo, Apie Begay, drawing sandpaintings with black and red crayolas in an effort to make them permanent. Shortly thereafter, Hosteen Klah, a noted medicine man, attempted the same thing by weaving sandpainting designs into the awkward medium of blankets. Many, mostly outsiders, continued to try to record sandpaintings but it was not until the technique of combining glue and sand on a board was developed that the Navajo themselves began to successfully preserve sandpaintings. The simplicity of the method and the availability of materials eventually produced an art form that retains one element of the traditional and another element that is widely divergent from the original that inspired it.

There is a hiatus of unknown length between the cliff art from the *Dinétah* and the next known examples of *Diné* art that appear on the cliffs of Canyon de Chelly and Canyon del Muerto in Arizona. The bright yellow painting of antelope at Antelope House and the well-known drawing of a procession of Spanish soldiers at Standing Cow Ruin in Canyon del Muerto are recognized as the work of a single Navajo man, Dibé Yazhi. These pictographs have the same bold rendering as the earlier petroglyphs of the *Dinétah,* but they are only a few of the renditions in the canyons. It is not known who made the idiosyncratic renderings of the constellations in the well-hidden planetaria, who pecked the symbols of the Monster Slayer twins, who produced the line of Ute warriors, or who created the multitudes of other drawings on the cliffs. They have survived because they were rendered in a medium more resistant to mislocation or destruction than other

ABOVE: *This striking example of an 1890s Germantown weaving, 63" by 67", demonstrates the Navajos' exuberance in design and color as new colors became available. The center section may have been inspired by Mexican Saltillo weavings, which were made in two sections and joined in the middle.*

FOLLOWING, PAGE 12: *This 8' by 6' Germantown rug, circa 1900, is from the John Lorenzo Hubbell–Ganado period and is made of aniline-dyed handspun yarn. The crosses with tufted corners are sometimes referred to as Spider Woman Crosses.*

FOLLOWING, PAGE 13: *A classic Navajo serape, circa 1860, 55" by 38".*

This 46" by 58 1/2" Navajo weaving, 1890–1910, is a Third Phase chief's blanket. More elaborate than the First and Second Phase styles, the Third Phase adds stepped triangles to the stripes that were common to the earlier chief's blankets.

forms. This is fortunate, as they represent an intermediate step that links later art with that of the *Dinétah*.

Understandably, sandpaintings and petroglyphs were not the only forms of drawing or painting, but both share an attribute that is a constant in early Navajo art, the lack of a developed background. In two-dimensional Euro-American art, the background is an essential part of the work, a setting in which the objects of interest are integrated. In early Navajo art, the background is not an essential part of the expression. It is a blank field where the image alone is important and carries the total content. This element is a almost a constant in the flat art of the Navajo.

In and around the Santa Fe area of New Mexico during the first decades of the twentieth century, there was a burgeoning interest in the art of Native Americans, primarily that of the Pueblos. Various Pueblo Indians like Fred Kabotie, a Hopi man, were recognized as artists of merit and their works were collected. In this fertile field, one individual in particular made an impact. Dorothy Dunn, a school teacher at Santo Domingo Pueblo Day School in the 1920s, had used art as an aid in teaching and was entranced with the efforts of her students. She subsequently left to complete her formal education at the Art Institute of Chicago, and when she returned her interest in Native art was re-doubled. Fortuitously, her return coincided with a change in government attitudes toward Native Americans and their schooling. With the help of several well-known Anglo artists, some politicians, and a few Indians, the Studio of Indian Art was established, and she became the teacher. How she taught and the amount of impact that her methods had on the students has been a subject of controversy through the years.

It is known that she encouraged the students to call upon their own traditions, and used many devices to further this process. At the same time, she had very definite ideas of what Indian art should look like, and in many instances, these were romantic, as could be expected in that era. In consequence, much of the material selected for inspiration was probably biased in that it was chosen because it looked as she felt Indian art should look. However, other elements were operating in her classes that are infrequently considered, among them the variation in tribes, the size and close-knit coherency of the group being taught, its introversion and degree of self-insemination. The recollections of members of the group, such as the Navajo artist Harrison Begay, tell of an overwhelming amount of interaction. There was no way they could escape exerting influence on one another's work. The success they achieved produced a style of painting that became known as "Traditional Indian Art." Almost all early twentieth-century Navajo art shows the impact of the style developed in this school. Traders in the business of selling Indian arts and crafts not only stocked this type of art work but tried to make sure that the supply continued, primarily by not buying anything that did not look like this stereotype.

In the decade following World War II, many Native American artists began to chafe under the economic yoke of the Indian traders and sought to expand their horizons, while at the same time, there was evidence that the demand for "Traditional Indian Art" was decreasing. There was resistance to change among some of the traders, although others supported the innovative artists. Sporadically, seminars aimed at the young Native American artists were promoted by different groups, and new shows were initiated that encouraged non-traditional art. Promising artists were also sponsored for art programs at universities and art schools to sharpen their skills. Through the curricula taught at each facility, the students learned from a different art tradition, one that would have increasing importance in their art.

Through the decades of the sixties and seventies, there was an increasing amalgamation with the methods and attitudes of Euro-American art and a dimunition of inspiration from the traditional. As the innovative efforts of these artists spread, there was an unleashing of restrictive tribal boundaries, a crossing-over of concepts between tribes, of borrowings and experimentations that produced a newer, more vibrant art. Navajo flat art blossomed during this period as subject matter expanded, new techniques were adopted, and innovative media were explored. In the same manner that the small group of students in Santa Fe had shared and developed a distinctive art form, so this much larger group of artists borrowed, incorporated, and reinforced each other, as open to change as had been the *Diné* in the distant past.

For the Navajo, however, the past is always a part of the present, and there is a constant harkening back to those beginnings. As Lois and Jerry Jacka present their informed selections of contemporary Navajo art, taking pleasure in each with the discrimination of connoisseurs, readers will find the lines between past and present blurring as they do for the the *Diné*. It is often difficult to tell whether the art presented here is old, foretelling a time yet to come, or contemporary, recalling the earlier elegance of the traditional, but the distinction is unnecessary as readers will undoubtedly enjoy the Jackas' trip through Navajo artistry.

THE NAVAJO WAY

ABOVE: Blessings from Female Rain, a 9 1/2" tall by 18" long sculpture of Utah alabastar by Alvin K. Marshall. "This sculpture represents the softness of the touch from Female Rain," the artist said. "She comes before the storm to prepare and comfort her children who belong to Mother Earth."

PREVIOUS PAGE: Yei'ii and Coyote Dances, a 40" by 32" mixed media by Redwing T. Nez. Talking God feeds corn pollen to Coyote (the Trickster) after overpowering him. The rectangular frame surrounded by stars represents eternity, and the blue, green, and red streaks are a whirling rainbow driven by the forces of the Four Winds: Big Wind, Skinny Wind, Gray Wind, and Dark Wind. The swirling colors surrounding Talking God signify the motion of the dances. "This painting is a visual chant," Redwing said. "When I'm left alone to work, this is what I come up with."

THE NAVAJO WAY

"This is where it all began." Redwing Nez swept an arm out toward the valley below the old

Bidahochi Trading Post where we stood on a chilly morning. With hair tied back into

the traditional Navajo hourglass bun wrapped with white yarn, the tall,

thirty-three-year-old Navajo painter grinned as he continued.

"Down there is where I herded sheep. Then I'd come up here to the trading post to sit and sketch. I didn't know that was 'art.' It was just a way to amuse myself. I sold the sketches to tourists for fifty cents each, then bought popsicles and pop in the trading post. It was great; I didn't have to ask anyone for money anymore.

"I'd find old *Horseman* magazines that had been thrown away—almost wore them out looking at the pictures over and over again. Sometimes I'd daydream until I felt like I was walking into a scene. I remember . . . "

I remember. Those words are repeated often by Navajo artists. And what most remember first is a reservation of almost sixteen million acres that sprawls across the vast reaches of the high plateau country of northeastern Arizona and northwestern New Mexico and nips up into southeast Utah. Set within an irregular diamond-shaped area, Navajoland is guarded by a sacred mountain in each of the Four Directions: Blanca Peak, East; Mt. Taylor, South; the San Francisco Peaks, West; and Mt. Hesperus, North.

This land is sacred to the *Diné* (the People, the name pre-ferred by the Navajo), around 200,000 of them who make up the largest tribe in the United States. They have persevered against tremendous odds, yet retained a lively, but quiet, sense of humor. They are resourceful, intelligent, adaptive, talented, innovative, deeply emotional, and very spiritual.

Much is sacred in their world—in fact, everything in the natural and super-natural world is sacred—yet there is no Navajo word for "religion." The term presents a foreign concept to the *Diné*. Their spirituality is as much a part of life as breathing, and the Navajo Way is just that: a way of life. It emphasizes cooperation, knowledge, and order, and centers around maintaining life's delicate balance between man, nature, and spirituality at all times. Thus they assure *hózhó*, a comprehensive word meaning beauty, perfection, well-being, blessings, order, good health, harmony—in short, the ideal environment. Ill health and all other misfortune occur as a result of disrupted harmony.

Through ritual, the traditional Navajo appeals to the Holy People to provide blessings and healing—physical, emotional, or mental—thereby restoring *hózhó*. Performed by a *hataałi* (singer, shaman, medicine man), these rituals include dry (sand) paintings, chants, the *yei'ii bichai* (performers who represent the Holy People), and many other elements necessary for a particular ceremony. Each must be executed correctly or further misfortune may befall both patient and practitioner. Spirituality and ritual are an integral part of the Navajo Way, sustaining the *Diné* so they may walk safely along the Trail of Beauty in happiness and harmony.

Spirituality is the lifeblood of Navajo art. As contemporary sandpainter Joe Ben Jr. said, "It's the medicine men who are the true artists. They must question and interpret. They must journey back within themselves. Artists are just doing what medicine men do."

Carl Taylor, an almost-ninety-year-old *hataałi* is a prime example. This patriarch of a large, talented family lives in a comfortable hogan near Indian Wells, Arizona. On an autumn afternoon, he shared reminiscences and explained portions of the Navajo Way as his son Herbert acted as interpreter. Carl also agreed to allow photography of some sacred objects because, he said, "It's important to me, too. I think that a hundred years from now, people should know about these things."

"These things" included pages from a notebook that Carl kept as a teenager. With no way to write the Navajo language, he created his own symbolic "picture language" in order to record the prayers and songs he needed to learn to become a medicine man. "It was so I could remember," he said. He took these priceless, seventy-year-old pieces of paper from a small, wrinkled paper bag.

He also allowed photography of objects he uses in ceremonies, such as flint, pollen, onyx, and small buckskin-wrapped "weapons"—symbolic of the weapons used by the Hero Twins to defeat their enemies. As he removed these sacred articles from a wedding basket, he said, "These things are used for being successful and against hard times, bad dreams—for healing."

Straining to see the dim images he had drawn so long ago on the old paper, he endeavored to explain their meaning in halting Navajo, at a disadvantage in trying to make a *bilagáana* understand. Herbert also had difficulty translating some of the explanations into English; there are simply no words for certain Navajo terms. Any problems with translation were not important; the cryptic code Carl had invented for his songs and prayers was fascinating. He smiled and

OPPOSITE: *Ceremonial objects from Carl Taylor's medicine bundle surround the tattered remnants of notes he made some seventy years ago when he was about seventeen. Carl used "pictographic" figures to record the prayers, songs, and chants he had to memorize in order to become a* hataałi. *The colored figures at lower left represent a healing prayer, and were interpreted by Carl as follows: the yellow is the sunrise followed by a* yei'ii *called Talking God, a second* yei'ii, *White Corn Boy, Yellow Corn Girl, Corn Pollen Boy, the planter (an insect), and the Holy Sky (blue color at far right). Carl's pictographic ceremonial "art" is similar to that pecked into or painted onto cliffs by his ancestors more than two centuries ago.*

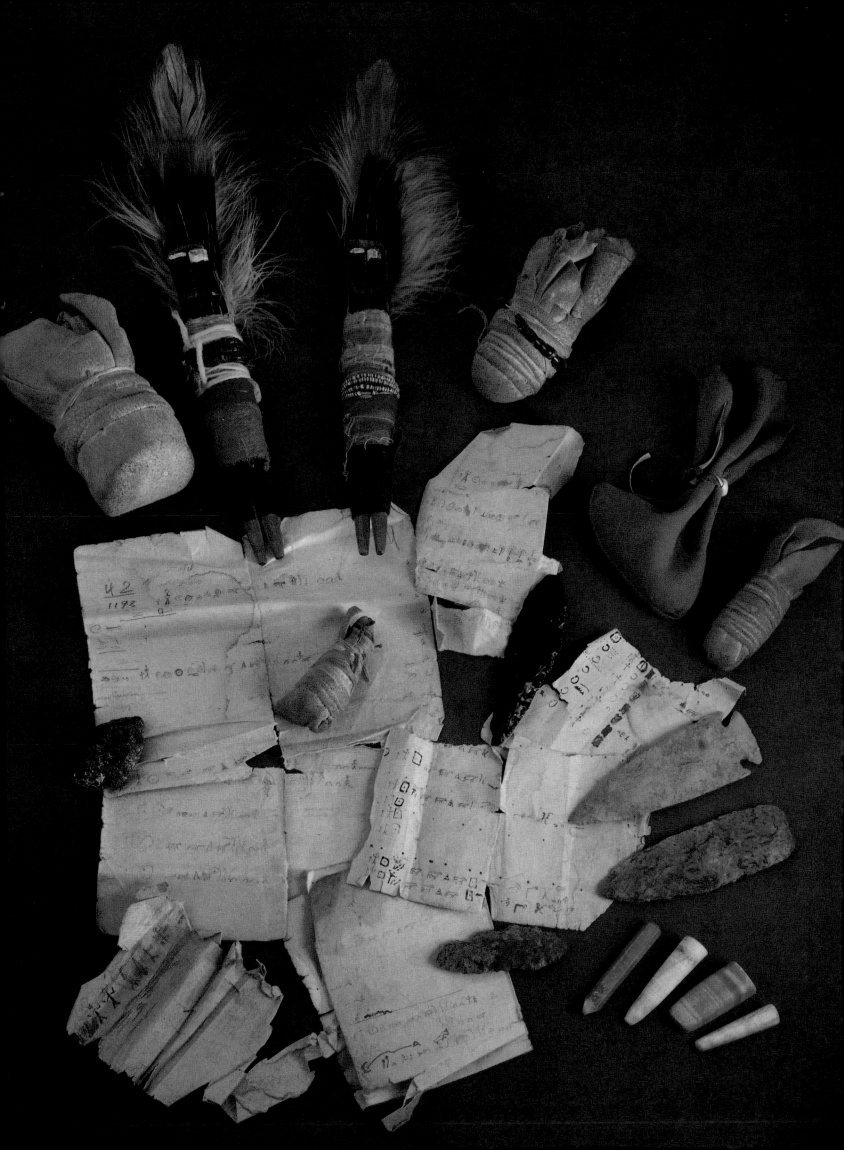

nodded, pleased when certain symbols were recognized after they were repeated several times: Talking God, sheep, the Center of Dawn.

Carl may have simply been taking notes as he studied to be a *hataałi* all those years ago, but he presented a priceless treasure by allowing us to share this portion of his walk along the Beauty Trail.

Life's trail may be likened to the walk around the inside of a ceremonial hogan. It is entered from the East—a place of new beginnings and spiritual reawakening. The color of the East is white, which symbolizes purity, divinity, and perfect ceremonial control. It is the morning of life—a time of hope, expectation, and promise, a time to set goals.

The walk proceeds clockwise to the South, which represents Day-Sky. Blue, the South's color, symbolizes the fruitfulness of the earth. It is a time of growth and learning to reason. Young people become involved in daily routine: receiving an education, developing a career, starting a family.

Upon reaching the West, the time of Evening-Twilight, one has achieved maturity. Life revolves around marriage, family, and home. The yellow color of the West symbolizes the power of pollen and other wild vegetation. It is twilight, a family time.

The North represents Night-Darkness, and its color is black, sinister and threatening. But by the time one reaches the North, he or she has grown old and wise; grandchildren are encouraged to remember the Old Way, to keep the traditions, and to take part in ceremonies. Darkness is a time for reflection and remembrance, a time to rest both mind and body, knowing that one has walked the trail in Beauty.

This glimpse into the artists' lives will follow a similar trail, as their art silently echoes memories of the traditional lifestyle, Native American symbolism, and the unique beauty of their homeland. Artists remember soft breezes whispering across sand dunes, the splendor of sunrises over rugged mountain peaks, summer storms thundering their way across the heavens, and the fragrance of rain-washed juniper. They have fond memories of sitting beside mothers, aunts, and grandmothers weaving at their looms, and watching fathers, grandfathers, uncles, and older brothers turn sheets of silver and chunks of raw turquoise into objects of beauty. They remember the timelessness of quiet, sandstone canyons and the magic of sitting alone among pinnacles and spires, of rising at dawn to pray to the Holy People in the East, and seeing the *yei'ii bichai* perform on star-studded winter nights. They remember tending grazing flocks, and listening to grandparents tell stories of the past and recount *Diné* legends.

Some also watched the sun rise over city skyscrapers, or sailed the seas to distant lands. Many attended universities or served in the military. There are those who were raised in an urban environment and others who now reside there; many artists have achieved success in this "outside world." Yet always, there is that other world—although it may be hundreds of miles and a lifetime away—the Navajo world that whispers, "You are *Diné*." And inevitably, their memories draw them back, both literally and figuratively, to their homeland for inspiration.

"I remember . . . "

MORNING-DAWN

Now Dawn is in Harmony

It is calling me

Now within, I am in Harmony

It is calling me

I am long-life Harmony

It is calling me

Before me it is blessed

Behind me it is blessed

Below me it is blessed

Above me it is blessed

All around me it is blessed

I am long-life happiness

In blessing I go about

Before me it is blessed as I go about

Behind me it is blessed as I go about

Below me it is blessed as I go about

Above me it is blessed as I go about

All around me is it blessed as I go about

I have become blessed again

I have become blessed again

—from The Blessingway

ABOVE: *A traditional wedding basket (13 1/2" diameter), woven by Christine King, is shown with a very contemporary basket olla (16 3/4" tall and 20 1/2" in diameter) by Elsie Holiday, who was inspired by one of Richard Zane Smith's pottery ollas that she saw in Beyond Tradition. This unusual piece won First Prize and a special award at the 1993 Gallup Intertribal Indian Ceremonial.*

PREVIOUS PAGE: Dawn Eternal, *24" by 20" inch pastel by Teddy Draper Jr. "It's early morning on the Navajo reservation," Teddy said, "at a place up in the red rocks about four or five miles west of Chinle. It's spring, and everything is fresh and new. There's no clutter around the hogan because the people are making a new beginning after the cold of winter. The snow is gone, but the stream is still trickling with the late run-off."*

MORNING-DAWN

A new day is dawning. Below the eastern horizon, the sun subtly flirts with the morning.

All is hushed and still. A hawk circles high above; the pungent fragrance of

juniper pervades the crisp, chilly air. A few wispy clouds

blush rosy-pink as the sky begins to lighten.

In Navajo country, the sun comes up, not like thunder, but gently like a soft breeze whispering across the sand dunes. As it finally peeks over the mountaintop, its golden rays streak upward toward Father Sky and its golden glow streams across Mother Earth spotlighting the sandstone pinnacles and spires scattered below.

Sheep rustle in pole corrals; dogs rise, yawning and stretching, ready to accompany herds once they are set free to graze. The People begin to stir; the scent of a juniper fire blends with that of fresh coffee brewing.

From east-facing hogan doorways, the traditional Navajo goes out to greet the dawn, to pray and make offerings to the Holy People. Long shadows silently creep across the land as the sun begins its westward journey through the heavens. It is morning: a time of spiritual reawakening, of renewal and hope. It is the springtime of life, a time to plan, to determine what one hopes to accomplish in the future.

To Navajo artists, this spiritual time brings memories of the Navajo Way, the ceremonies, the Holy People. It is a time of new beginnings, a time when adolescents join the ranks of artists, when traditional art begins to take on new aspects, when outside influences appear in an artist's work.

The majority of Navajo artists lived the Navajo Way as children, and many continue to do so. Others, who were perhaps reared in urban areas, often spent summers with reservation

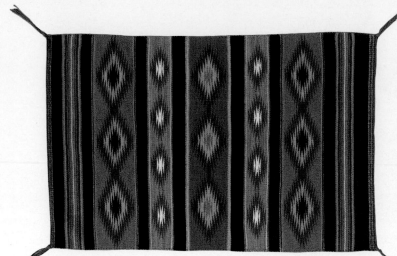

This 19" by 29" Wide Ruins style rug, woven by sixteen-year-old Celesly Shabi, was awarded First Prize and Best of Show in the Young Artist's Category at the 1991 Navajo Nation Fair. Wide Ruin rugs are characterized by both broad and narrow stripes of plain color interspersed with bands of geometric designs (often diamonds) and narrower bands with more delicate motifs. Traditional Wide Ruins colors tend toward earth tones, but weavers are now adding some brighter colors.

grandparents. Most seem to share similar memories—of listening to ancient legends and stories of the old ways, of attending healing ceremonies, of learning their traditions and the intricacies of the Navajo Way.

It is these memories that inevitably provide inspiration. Fact becomes fantasy as a way of life is recreated and transformed with the clank of chisel on stone. Fantasy becomes fact as life is breathed into stories and legends with the stroke of brush on canvas.

Many artists excel in more than one medium. Sculptors may also be painters, weavers may be silversmiths, silversmiths may be painters. And a painter may work in such diverse styles that it is difficult to imagine that the paintings were done by just one person. Although artistic talent seems to be an inherent trait, the *Diné* culture also tends to propagate artists. Art comes very easily to these talented people, but why they are so prolific is another matter.

Economics, of course, play a very large role, and the seemingly insatiable fascination with "Indians" and their art, both in this country and abroad, promises a steady market. As a youngster, Redwing Nez wondered just why there was this interest in Native American art. "I was sitting in a sweathouse one time with Kee Hosteen, a *hataałi*," Redwing said. "I ask him, 'How come those whites like to buy our things?' The old man said, 'Those white people, they're water people. Their hearts and minds are clear, so they like things that are shiny and bright. They have to have a lot of decoration. They decorate their bodies, but their souls need something. Their souls enjoy your art. That's why you can sell it.' "For generations, the majority of the *Diné* have depended upon some form of arts and crafts for at least part of their livelihood. Employment opportunities are scarce on the reservation, and young people who leave home to attend schools of higher learning frequently find it difficult to utilize their newly acquired skills in their homeland.

"It beats the hell out of driving a truck or riding a bronc." —GIBSON NEZ

Art not only provides a livelihood, but is something they enjoy doing. It is also a means of competing, even "mastering," the uncertainties of the "outside world." While many say that art is a way of preserving their culture, pragmatic master-jeweler Gibson Nez says succinctly and honestly, "It beats the hell out of driving a truck or riding a bronc."

However, the *Diné* value skills above wealth, and accumulating riches is a foreign concept. Good fortune or periods of prosperity are simply opportunities to share with family. The desire to create objects of beauty is deeply ingrained, and there is pride in accomplishment.

Contrary to what one may hear, "Indian art" is not gasping its last breath.

Bruce Burnham, of Burnham Trading Post in Sanders, Arizona, declared emphatically, "It [weaving] is not a dying art; it is alive and changing constantly. There are more talented weavers today than ever before and, within the next ten years, we're going to see more exciting weaving than ever before. If it's a dying art, why are so many of the weavers young?"

"My mother would send me over to my grandmother's to borrow sugar or potatoes, but Grandma would make me card thirty-one batts of wool before she would give me the food."—SARAH PAUL BEGAY

This black soapstone sculpture, 12" tall, was created by eighteen-year-old Lance Yazzie. Taught to carve by his father, sculptor Larry Yazzie, Lance began working with stone when he was thirteen and is now noted for his carvings of bears. The bear is a central figure in Navajo lore and legend, and an important part of the Spirit World.

Although Bruce spoke specifically of weaving, his statement is true of all Navajo art. Multitudes of young people are involved in all mediums, and new artists continue to appear on the scene.

The expectations of elders undoubtedly have something to do with this phenomenon. It is anticipated that children will be creative. They are encouraged to experiment with all types of art and, almost from the cradleboard, their talents are nutured. They are urged to "make something" from clay, or to weave pieces of yarn onto small cardboard "looms," or to draw on anything—paper bags, cardboard boxes, pieces of wood.

"I was always drawing," Wallace Begay said. "There were always stacks of dried wood around. They made a great surface. I drew all over them."

"It's difficult to say just when I decided I wanted to be an artist," Jack To'Baahe Gene said. "It's just always been there." Although different words

ABOVE LEFT: *"Transitional" style rug woven by Nina Beno. This 65" by 72" rug was copied from an old painting of an 1890s rug at Hubbell Trading Post. The turn of the century was a period of time when chief's blankets were evolving into other styles.*

ABOVE RIGHT: *Like her mother, Nina, sixteen-year-old Cheryl Beno often weaves replicas of older rugs. This 19" by 30" rug, an "old style" Ganado that was popular around the turn of the century, won Second Prize in the Young Artist's Category at the 1991 Navajo Nation Fair Arts and Crafts Exposition.*

were used, the artists all expressed basically the same sentiments time and time again.

Weaver Sarah Paul Begay laughed as she explained the "nurturing" tactics used by her family. "My mother would send me over to my grandmother's to borrow sugar or potatoes, but Grandma would make me card thirty-one batts of wool before she would give me the food. The next time I came, she would make me spin the batts into yarn. Then every time I went to her house, I would have to weave. I was about six years old; I sold my first rug when I was seven." Sarah shook her head and smiled. "It wasn't a very pretty sight to see. It was made from the wool Grandma made me card. But I learned."

According to legend, the gift of weaving was given to the *Diné* through the Spider People. After Spider Man and Spider Woman named the weaving tools, Spider Man said, "From now on when a baby girl is born, you shall go and find a spider web woven at the mouth of some hole; you must take it and rub it on the baby's hand and arm. Then, when she grows up, she will weave, and her fingers will not tire." (Aileen O'Bryan, *Navaho Indian Myths,* 1993) Changing Woman, who first learned to weave from Spider Woman, taught the skill to the *Diné.*

Since the Spider People were a *Kiis'aani,* or Pueblo group, one might conclude that the legend agrees with recorded history, which says that the Navajos learned to weave from the Puebloans. Legend and history aside, the *Diné* became master of the craft and have long been noted for their weaving. A few schools, such as Navajo Community College, offer a weaving class or two, but this art is usually learned from grandmothers, mothers, and aunts.

In order to allow more time at the loom, many weavers combine homespun yarn with the excellent commercially processed yarns available today; others rely on the latter entirely. This in no way lessens the quality of their weaving; it is simply a practical choice.

The weaver who processes her own wool spends many hours in preparation. Sheep are tended year round and sheared in the spring, then the wool is washed and dried, carded into batts, handspun, and dyed; the sturdy upright loom must be prepared and the warp yarn positioned. Each process is very time consuming.

Weaving is also a slow, tedious task and, given the time spent in preparation and in weaving, many weavers in the past were fortunate to make minimum wages. But things are changing and, as Bill Malone, manager of Hubbell Trading Post, says, "It's about time! The world has treated weaving as a craft for much too long. The better weavers today are going for works of art and are finally getting the recognition they deserve as artists." Even though this recognition and its accompanying raise in income are important, personal satisfaction and social rewards are still the primary force behind Navajo weaving. Caring for relatives, which includes clan members as well as actual kinsmen, is one of the first priorities of the Navajo, so the weaver's contribution not only adds to the family coffers, but earns prestige.

Traditionally, certain songs and prayers accompany each weaving, tribal taboos are avoided, and ritual directives are obeyed. These practices have led to two common misconceptions about weaving. One is that a "mistake" is, for various reasons, included in each rug. No one seems to know where this myth began, but trader Bill Malone (who is not only married to a Navajo weaver but has worked with hundreds of them) says the often-repeated statement is untrue. "The idea that weavers purposely make a mistake in each rug is a fallacy," he declared. "That story was probably invented by some trader to excuse the poor rugs he was trying to sell."

One who knows even a little about the Navajo Way would be skeptical of this tale. Weavers express beauty while creating harmony within, a harmony

BELOW: *Seven-year-old Finnia Lynn Begay (better known as Pumkin) wove these two rugs when she was only five—and she continues to improve with age. They are 12" by 14" and 9 1/2" by 11" in size.*

OPPOSITE: *This exceptional rug, which is 10' by 6 1/2', was woven by Sarah Paul Begay. It includes twenty-four different rug styles and 130 colors. Sarah spent 979 hours at the loom, plus additional time in wool preparation, in creating this masterpiece.*

achieved by blending diverse elements in a pleasing way. Therefore, it is highly unlikely that any weaver would purposely create disorder, but, as one weaver said, "She might just make a mistake and leave it in rather than go to the trouble of redoing hours of work."

The contrasting line commonly woven through one corner of a rug's border has also led to numerous misinterpretations of the reasons for its inclusion, probably due to the difficulty of explaining the abstract cultural concepts to a non-Navajo. In fact, misunderstanding the Navajo language may have been responsible for old-time traders coining the incorrect terms "spirit line" and "devil's pathway"—or else they simply needed a colorful tale for the tourists.

It is a difficult concept to explain to a non-Navajo, but D. Y. Begay tried. "When interpreted literally," she said, "the Navajo word for the line is 'a trail' or 'a way out.' It has nothing to do with evil spirits; there is nothing evil about it. Nor is it for good spirits. It is for us [weavers]. Sometimes my mind gets so totally taken up with weaving that I can't think of anything else. When both mind and body become so absorbed, a weaver may become trapped. We add the line to give us 'a way out.' "

"The better weavers today are going for works of art and are finally getting the recognition they deserve as artists."—BILL MALONE

In *A Guide to Navajo Rugs* (Southwest Parks and Monuments Association, 1992), weaver Mae Jim is quoted on this subject. "You leave a line going in and out again. Your design is your thinking, so you don't border that up. It's your home and all that you have. And so if you close that up, you close everything up—even your thinking and your work."

Some weavers refer to this as having "cobwebs on the brain," and many, but not all, continue to include what might be more appropriately called the "weaver's trail" or "pathway" to avoid this affliction.

There is great diversity today in rug styles, designs, and colors. Those that exhibit a particular regional style—Ganado, Wide Ruins, Burntwater, Teec Nos Pos, and others—may have been woven anywhere, and designs of one style may be combined with colors traditionally used in another.

A prime example is the New Lands rug, which combines the intricacies of the Teec Nos Pos design with Burntwater colors in a raised-outline technique. Although the raised-outline rug was common among Coal Mine Mesa weavers, bright colors and bold patterns were normally used. When many weavers from that area were relocated to Sanders as a result of the Navajo-Hopi land dispute, Bruce Burnham of Burnham Trading Post began encouraging them to retain the raised-outline technique, but use more muted colors in weaving the complex Teec Nos Pos designs.

"Most of the weavers didn't want to trouble with the task of learning something new," Bruce said, "but Wanda Begay was young and eager to experiment. She was the first to begin experimenting with the New Lands style. She deserves the credit for developing it."

Wanda Begay is credited with developing the New Lands style rug, which combines Teec Nos Pos designs with Burntwater colors using the raised outline technique. This intricate rug is 102" by 63".

Traders have had a very positive influence on weaving over the years and, even today, there are those who still work with weavers in the old way. Sometimes they offer suggestions for new designs or colors; at other times they encourage weavers to try their own innovations. They often furnish financial assistance, which can run into thousands of dollars, to a weaver during the months it takes to complete a special rug.

Sarah Paul Begay excels at producing special weavings. After a dream in which her grandmother showed her a new design, Sarah sketched out the idea and began. Nine hundred and seventy-nine working hours later (not counting the time spent in wool preparation), she had completed a six-and-a-half by ten foot masterpiece. One hundred and thirty different colors were incorporated into twenty-four different weaving styles.

The weaving tradition continues, generation after generation, and Sarah Begay is now teaching her five daughters to weave. Seven-year-old Finnia Lynn (or "Pumkin"), who is the youngest artist included in this publication, began her lessons when she was just two-and-a-half.

"Whatever else I become, I will always be a weaver. And I plan to teach the daughter I hope to have one day."—JENNIFER MUSIAL

As a toddler, Jennifer Musial, now age eighteen, watched her mother, noted weaver Kalley Keams Musial, at the loom. She was given a piece of cardboard with strings attached for practicing, but by the time she was five, had graduated to an upright loom. Jennifer sees weaving as "an art form to express oneself," and adds that "rugs are all just feelings. When my spirits are high, I use lighter colors; when I'm feeling a little low, I tend to go with darker ones. A lot depends on what's going on around me."

Jennifer, who has won numerous awards, plans to be a child psychologist but says, "Whatever else I become, I will always be a weaver. And I plan to teach the daughter I hope to have one day." Jennifer's weaving, *Seasons of Change,* defies

The prize-winning contemporary weavings of Kalley Keams Musial and her eighteen-year-old daughter, Jennifer, are a style unto themselves and are woven with all vegetal-dyed yarns. Kalley and Jenny often travel to museums across the country to demonstrate their weaving techniques. The 21 1/2" by 32" rug by Jennifer, Seasons of Change *(right), won First Prize in the Youth Division at the 1993 Santa Fe Indian Market. Kalley's rug (below) is 18 1/2" by 27".*

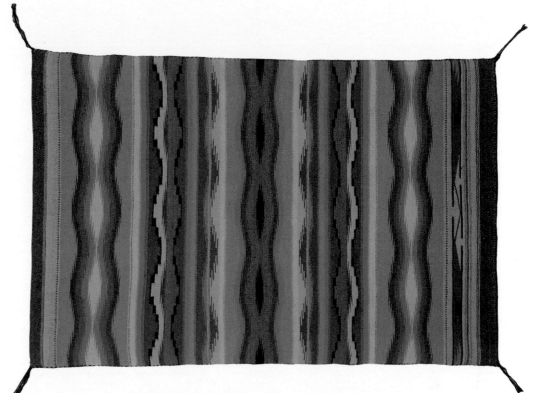

classification; it is simply a beautiful work of art created by a talented young artist who successfully blends modern society and the "other world" she enters when she sits before the loom.

"I'll never know it all, but I try to listen and learn, and my sculpture is now a very spiritual thing to me."—ROY WALTERS

Jimmy Abeita's Sandpainter *demonstrates one of the earliest forms of Navajo art. In this 24" by 30" oil on canvas, a* hataałi *creates a sandpainting during a healing ceremony.*

IN THE *DINÉ* WORLD, where "all good things come from the East with the Dawn," Morning is a time of spiritual reawakening. Jesse Monongye remembers rising with the dawn as a youngster to go out with his grandmother to pray. "I'd shuffle along through the snow, bleary-eyed, shoes untied, carrying the basket with the pollen in it," he says with a chuckle. "I'd say, 'Why can't we stay in the hogan and pray today? Why can't we just pray for ourselves instead of the whole world? Why do we have to pray so early?' My grandmother said, 'We have to say our prayers early so God can hear them before all those white people get up and start praying. There's more of them.'"

Many Navajos today find that the Native American Church, which combines the rituals and tenets of the Old Way with those of Christianity, fulfills their

This intricate 24" by 24" sandpainting, *Mother Earth / Father Sky. It was awarded*
Ten Day Chant, *is Rosie Yellowhair's inter-* *First Prize and Best of Class, plus a Special*
pretation of ten different ceremonial designs: *Award, at the 1993 Gallup Intertribal*
Whirling Feather, Creation Story, Whirling *Indian Ceremonial.*
Log, Ribbon Dance-Earth, Sun Creation,
Water Creatures, Frogs with Sacred Plants,
Sky People Dancer, Home of the Yei'iis, and

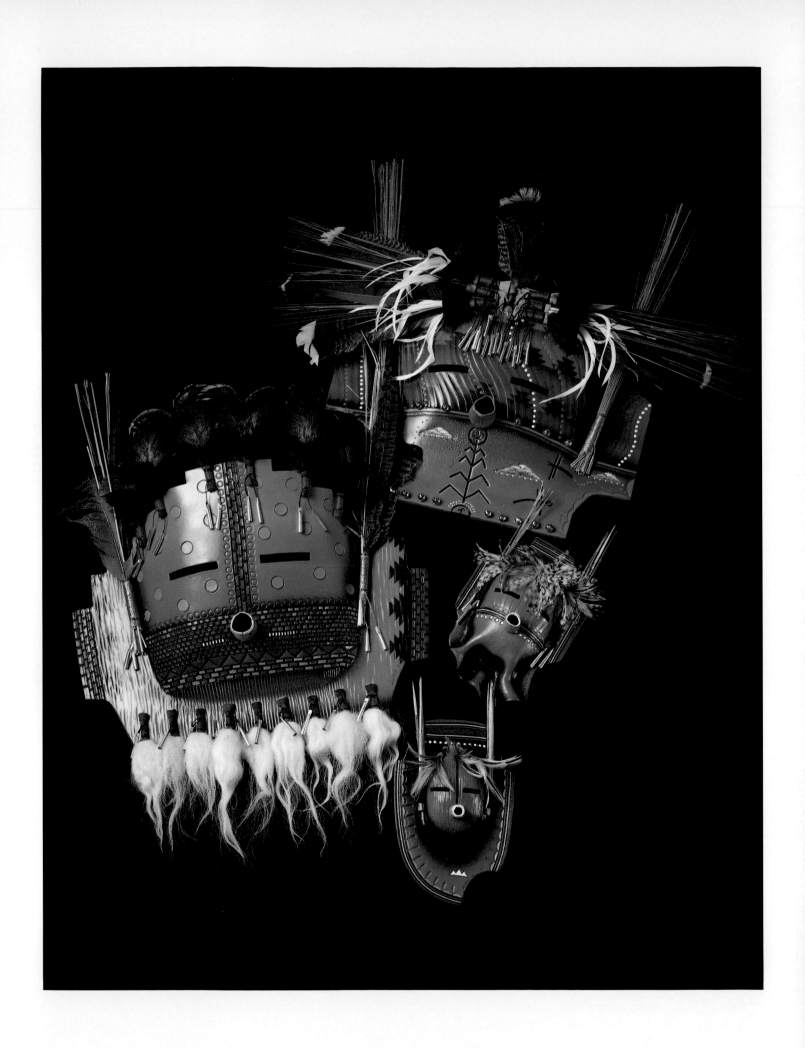

ABOVE: *David K. John (not to be confused with David Johns) painted this 42" by 36" acrylic on canvas of* Talking God Yei'ii, *the deity who is considered the Grandfather of the Diné.*

OPPOSITE: *Ceramic masks by Peter Ray James are the artist's contemporary interpretation of Navajo deities. Ranging in length from 10" to 26", they are titled (clockwise from left)* Grandmother to the Basketmakers, Summertime Enchantment, Contemplation, *and* Little Guardian.

ABOVE: Ceremonial Expression, *a 23" by 35" ballpoint pen drawing by Johnson Charley, received First Prize at the 1993 Gallup Intertribal Indian Ceremonial.*

LEFT: *Ryan Benally (Haskéya-Teh-Des-Wod) is a sixteen-year-old sculptor who demonstrates the skill and sensitivity of a much older artist. This alabaster sculpture, Desert Flower, is 21 1/2" tall.*

OPPOSITE: Chanter, *a 24 1/2" tall alabaster sculpture by Tim Washburn.*

spiritual needs. Peyote is only one ceremonial element of this belief; there are also four main principles to observe: family responsibility, self-reliance, love for one's fellowman, and abstention from alcohol use.

Roy Walters credits the Native American Church with turning his life around. "I had a lot of shortcomings," he admitted. "Then in 1988, I became very spiritual. I joined the Native American Church and accepted their philosophies and teachings. I'll never know it all, but I try to listen and learn, and my sculpture is now a very spiritual thing to me."

The Holy People are very much a part of Navajo life. Purification or healing ceremonies include the use of herbs, songs, prayers, and dry (sand) paintings. Depending upon the patient's illness and its cause, a particular portion of Navajo legend is recounted and sandpaintings are created by the *hataałi* or his assistants. Lured by their likeness, the Holy People portrayed enter the sandpainting, or *'iikááh,* "the place where Deities come and go." The patient sitting upon the sandpainting becomes one with the Holy People for a time as their power enters his body to provide strength and healing. Due to their tremendous power, the Deities cannot remain in this state; the sandpainting is scattered upon completion of the ceremony and a new one is created each time.

"This art form bridges the gap between the spiritual world and the art world."

——PETER RAY JAMES

The *yei'ii bichai,* representing the Holy People, also appear at certain ceremonies. Due to their significance, the *yei'iis* are a prominent subject in Navajo art. Peter Ray James creates his own interpretation of these Holy People with his colorful ceramic masks. When asked if the elders object to his choice of art styles, Peter shook his head. "No, I thought they might, but they actually encouraged me. The masks are very contemporary work and they felt that I was attempting to translate with it. This art form bridges the gap between the spiritual world and the art world."

Wayne Beyale also combines art and spirituality when he adds a line or lines leading to the edge of each painting that includes a *yei'ii.* "Sandpaintings must be destroyed," Wayne explained, "because Navajo tradition and mythology teaches that permanent drawings would acquire too much power to be entrusted to the *Diné.* While it's easy to erase a sandpainting, permanent drawings on cloth, hides, or paper are not allowed unless the images are unfinished or there is some way for the *yei'iis* to escape."

Fidel Bahe related an experience that led him to use the "way out" in his jewelry. "I had just made a nice belt to enter in Gallup's Ceremonial, but I didn't get it done on time. Then my grandfather died, so I cut the belt in half and took a concho off the back and put it in with my grandfather. But I couldn't seem to work after that. Finally a medicine man told me it was because my mind was in the ground with my grandfather and we would have to sing it out. I knew that I

ABOVE: Firekeepers, *a 24" by 33" mixed media on rice paper by Mary Morez, depicts yei'iis and a horse, which the artist says "represents Fire God's horse. I included him because horses have great meaning and value among the Navajo, who are great horsemen."*

LEFT: *Jewelry by Tommy Jackson. This double-exposure photograph shows a gold and coral bracelet and necklace, and both sides of a reversible pendant. The beads and single stone are angel-skin coral combined with an overlay rug design. Multiple stones are inlaid to create a sun face, a cross, and a feathered fan on the reverse side of the pendant.*

OPPOSITE: *The yei'ii in relief on this metal sculpture by Tony Lee is forged of bronze; the 36" by 25" copper background has Navajo rug designs etched into the surface. After shaping and welding the pieces together, the sculpture was sand blasted. The patined finish is accomplished by applying the heat of a torch and chemicals simultaneously.*

ABOVE: *Noted for his exceptional tufacast work, Ric Charlie incorporates yei'ii figures and Navajo landscapes into silverwork that is enhanced by colored patinas. The box with a hinged top is made of six cast pieces soldered together; a male and female yei'ii grace the belt buckle, which has a cast Monument Valley landscape on the other side.*

RIGHT: *The technique used by Patrick Smith in making this hollowform or box-style jewelry results in very light-weight pieces with a massive look. The silver bracelet at top right represents a Hopi kachina. Heat was applied with a torch to produce the coloration of the highly polished "mild steele" headdress (tableta). The ring set with garnets (lower left) represents the headdress of an Apache Ghan dancer. The textures of the circular bracelet (lower right) were achieved by the reticulation technique. Settings include lapis lazuli, red and pink coral, turquoise, and lavulite.*

Designs on pottery made by Lucy Leuppe McKelvey and her three daughters are adapted from sandpaintings as well as other Navajo and Anasazi designs. From left to right are a gourd-shaped vessel (14" tall) by Cecilia, age twenty; a wedding vase (16" tall) by Celeste, eighteen; and a jar (15" tall) with sculpted Anasazi pueblo by Lucy. Above the pueblo are thundercloud and lightning designs and to the far right are ancient flute players. Celinda, sixteen, made the turtle canteen (10" long) set with turquoise.

would want to honor others of my family in this same way, so I asked 'How do I do this? Do I have to have prayers done every time?' But the medicine man said 'Leave an opening in your designs so you can get your thoughts and ideas back.' Since then, I always leave an opening."

The ritual "incomplete circle" is also used quite often in designs on pottery, baskets, and sandpaintings. To avoid sacrilege, artists of contemporary sandpaintings alter colors and designs, or may simply create their own interpretive patterns.

Some wonder exactly how to classify sandpaintings in the Native American art world. When Rosie Yellowhair was awarded first prize in the Fine Arts category at the 1991 Gallup Intertribal Indian Ceremonial, it was the first time in the event's seventy-year history that a sandpainting earned this honor. Knowing that many people don't consider sandpainting a fine art, Rosie was gratified.

"Sandpainting is a lot of work," Rosie said. "Even getting the sand and processing it is difficult and time-consuming. I get some sand from Cuba [New Mexico], the white sand from the Albuquerque area, the red from near Crown Point, the black comes from right along the road near the coal company, the

Ceremonial Run, *a 19" by 35" gouache and ink by Beverly Blacksheep, was awarded First Prize and Best of Category at the 1993 Gallup Intertribal Indian Ceremonial.*

turquoise is just turquoise ground up. I use rock chisels, hammers, and a grinder. The sand has to be ground several times before it's fine enough. I'll work on white sand for a full day to get enough to last about six months.

"The sand is sprinkled onto particle board covered with a mastic. Two layers of sand are used for the background; the second layer is smoothed by pressing it with paper. I paint the designs with a paintbrush dipped in glue, then the proper colored sand is sprinkled on. I like to do sandpaintings which have meaning for me."

Peter Nelson's jewelry also has meaning. "As a kid," he said, "I remember hauling water and riding horses, and I find myself including those designs in my work." Raised in the White Cone area of the reservation, Peter is the eldest of eleven children. His brother is an artist, three sisters and his mother are weavers, and one sister is learning to be a silversmith.

He attended the Institute of American Indian Art (IAIA) in Santa Fe, New Mexico, intending to pursue a painting career, but he also studied jewelry-making and soon decided it was the medium he preferred. "After I left the institute," Peter said, "I just sort of learned the rest on my own. In fact, the domed shadowbox style came about as a result of a mistake. I was hammering a piece for overlay and got too much of a rise in it. But I decided I like it."

"I'm not very interested in contemporary, mainstream, conceptual art. . . . I realize that this type of art comes from different ideas, personalities, and concepts, but it's difficult for me to fit them into an enduring art world."—TONY ABEYTA

Patrick Smith, with no plans to become a full-time artist, worked on a business administration degree at the University of Arizona, Tucson. However, both his brother and his father, Edison Smith (a noted traditional silversmith), urged him to do jewelry. Patrick changed his major to jewelry/silversmithing and he now is one of the top metalsmiths. More versed in metallurgy than most jewelers, he says "I do a lot of experimenting. Mokumé is a process which requires three

LEFT: *Peter Nelson's jewelry is of an unusual shadowbox style. The design is cut out of a sheet of silver, then slightly domed, separating it from the piece of oxidized silver to which it is soldered. His jewelry includes geometric and Navajo lifestyle designs.*

RIGHT: *The unique jewelry of Fidel Bahe. Except for the buckle (lower left), which has added texture, these pieces show the natural texture of tufastone. This technique involves carving the desired design and shape into the tufastone, which becomes the mold for the casting process. The buckle at top right has three elevations. The raised polished design represents a shooting star and the indented design with Royston turquoise represents a yei'ii. Turquoise in the remaining pieces is China Mountain.*

ABOVE: *The influence of Nathan Begaye's half-Hopi heritage is revealed in his work. However, Nathan says most of his designs come from clouds. "The open space on a pot is the sky itself. In fact, if a pot didn't have a border, the design would go on forever." These pieces range from miniatures as small as 1 1/4" tall to a vase 9" tall.*

RIGHT: *Jewelry by Jake Livingston. One necklace and ring set contains Nevada blue turquoise, the other coral. The coral and turquoise bracelet shows the influence of Jake's Zuni heritage. The eagle is inlaid with mother-of-pearl and engraved black pin shell.*

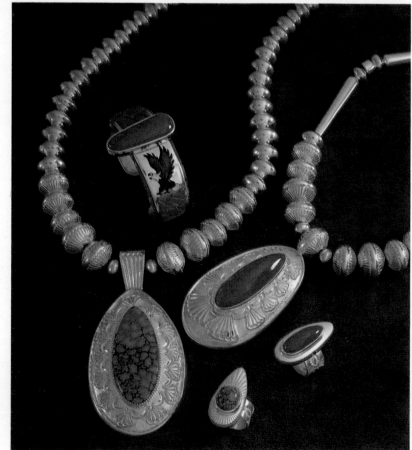

base metals. Gold, silver, and copper are melted together. Then I roll it out, cut it in half, and put one piece on top of the other. I keep doing that until I have twelve layers. It makes a really nice look." Patrick also uses a hollowform or box technique, which makes his jewelry appear massive and heavy in spite of its light weight.

"I woke up knowing I had to make pottery."——NATHAN BEGAYE

ALTHOUGH MORNING IS A TIME of new beginnings, beginnings are nothing new to the Navajo. They are a very adaptable people, yet it has always been selective adaptation. They conformed only when it would benefit them, learned only when something was of interest; anything else was ignored.

They learned farming from the Puebloans, but didn't choose to adopt their village way of life. They "acquired" sheep and cattle from the Spaniards, but had no desire to share their religion. Silversmithing was learned from Mexicans, weaving from Puebloans, but the Navajos were quick to add their own characteristics to each, making these arts their own. They were forced to submit to incarceration, but they never surrendered culturally.

In fact, Joe Ben Jr. says, "We never surrendered as a whole. Eight thousand of our people were forced to make the 'Long Walk' to Bosque Redondo where they were held for four years, but even more of them escaped into remote canyons and mountain areas even farther away. All of the people at Bosque Redondo were finally released and returned to our homeland. We were never really beaten!"

Although their present culture has been influenced by many different peoples, the *Diné* have never relinquished their own identity. They have absorbed other people into their society without sacrificing the Navajo Way; the lifestyle has changed over the years, but cultural precepts remain constant. Uninterested in the avant-garde, Navajo artists, too, assimilate only the best, not relying on gimmickery in their art.

Tony Abeyta, who does colorful and very powerful interpretive paintings of the sacred *yei'ii,* says "I'm not very interested in contemporary, mainstream, conceptual art. It has its own audience of thinkers, collectors, and critics. I consider myself a much more conservative traditionalist. I have a hard time appreciating a conceptual idea of filling a gallery with dirt and suspending car parts from the ceiling. I realize that this type of art comes from different ideas, personalities, and concepts, but it's difficult for me to fit them into an enduring art world."

Navajo art has endured for generations, and will continue to do so. However, there are many outside influences: modern society, other artists, and people of other tribes and nationalities. Perhaps the ones most affected by the latter are those with a parent who married outside the tribe. Even among neighboring tribes, cultural differences can be significant.

In mixed-tribal marriages, children may be reared in either culture; however, most southwestern tribes are matrilineal, so children are members of the mother's clan. When born to a Navajo father and non-Indian mother, a child has no primary clan identity.

Children from mixed marriages often suffer in one respect or another, but some artists have turned what might be a liability into an asset. Combining two cultures seems to have made them outstanding artists.

Nathan Begaye, Navajo-Hopi, says he was an introvert who often felt rejected by members of both tribes. Consequently, he spent much time alone, picking up broken shards of pottery and watching the clouds. "They were always changing and I could see things in them," he said. He learned to make pottery after a dream in which the setting sun and sky were bright red. He walked alone through abandoned Hopi villages until he came to a house where an old woman sat beside a fire surrounded by pots. "As I walked in," Nathan said, "she picked one up and handed it to me. I woke up knowing I had to make pottery." With the encouragement of his Hopi grandfather and his Navajo grandmother, Nathan began making pottery on his own. Later, he attended the IAIA, where he studied under his Hopi aunt Otellie Loloma. Today, his pottery reflects his intertribal heritage.

"I've always been a painter. There's never been any other choice. And I like the idea of being defined as a contemporary Indian painter. I've never been at rest with wanting to be an artist first who happens to be Indian."—TONY ABEYTA

Jesse Monongye's mother was Navajo and his father, Preston Monongye, although raised as a Hopi and accepted by most as a noted Hopi jeweler, was, in fact, of Mexican and Mission Indian ancestry. Although it is unusual for Navajo children not to be assimilated into some part of the tribal family, two-year-old Jesse, a three-year-old sister, and a five-year-old brother were abandoned because of their mixed heritage. However, they eventually returned to the reservation to live with distant kin, who became family. Jesse was grown before he met his father, who taught him to make jewelry. Jesse is now known for an intricate inlay style that many try to imitate but none have mastered. He has managed to overcome not only his most-inauspicious beginnings, but drug and alcohol abuse, as well, to become one of the top Indian artists in the country today.

Jake Livingston, Navajo-Zuni, combines two heritages in his stunning jewelry. "I was raised a Navajo," he says, "but I can speak both languages. My parents were both silversmiths and I picked it up from them." His uncle was the renowned Zuni silversmith, Dennis Edaakie, from whom Jake must also have "picked up" a few things. His exceptional jewelry combines Zuni inlay designs and other fine lapidary work with the massive look of Navajo jewelry.

Andy and Michael Kirk are brothers who bring yet another aspect of Indian culture into Navajo art. Children of a Navajo father and an Isleta Pueblo mother, they were raised, and still live, at the New Mexican pueblo. That culture is the only one they know, and both say that their inspiration comes from Pueblo spiritual beliefs and way of life. Defying categorization, their jewelry can only be described as magnificent.

OPPOSITE: *Wallace N. Begay created this unique 30" by 22" mixed media (acrylics and playing cards) based on the Edvard Munch classic,* The Scream. *The cards and money represent gambling on reservations and Native Americans "selling themselves" and their cultures.*

ABOVE: *Gary Lee's "paintings" are done by trickling colored sand through his hand as traditional sandpainters do. A warrior on horseback rides through the snow in this unusual 16" by 16" piece entitled* Buffalo Warrior. *The misty breath from the horse's nostrils was created by lightly wafting the dust from sifted sand across the painting.*

OPPOSITE: *One of the talented children of the noted painter Narciso P. Abeyta, Elizabeth Abeyta (Nah-Glee-eh-bah) has captivated the Native American art world with her unique, whimsical clay sculptures. Many of her figures portray Navajo life and Diné legends; others come from Aztec and Pueblo cultures. These sculptures range in height from 12" to 20 1/2".*

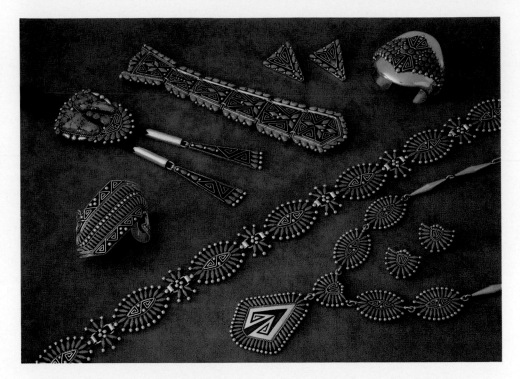

Cheryl Yestewa, Navajo-Hopi, is one who knew little about either of her native cultures. "I was born at Hopi, but raised in Phoenix," she explained. "I visited Oraibi in the summers. I guess I'm what could be called an 'apple,' red on the outside, white on the inside." She laughed as she made the remark, then added rather pensively, "I've always resented it a little that my parents didn't teach me more about my heritage."

Elizabeth and Tony Abeyta are the offspring of a Navajo-Anglo marriage. Their Navajo father, painter Narciso Abeyta, is noted for his unique art style, which drew the attention of Dorothy Dunn, a prime mover in Indian art of the early part of the twentieth century. "My father was not only a noted artist, but the first in his family to receive a college education," Elizabeth said. "As a translator for the tribe, he became more and more contemporized. Ironically, it was my [Anglo] mother's strong love for Navajo culture that gave me a more traditional outlook. She was a potter and was always dragging the seven of us kids off to dig for clay," Elizabeth chuckled. "We sort of lived in our own isolated world, and we always played with clay." Yet when Elizabeth considered working with handicapped children as a career choice, it was her father who suggested she pursue art instead. She attended Navajo Community College before moving on to IAIA, then to the San Francisco Art Institute. Fortunately, at each of those schools, Elizabeth was encouraged to "do her own thing." Today, her unique, whimsical clay sculptures have earned a place for her in the forefront of the art world. But always, Elizabeth remembers. "Some of my fondest memories are of times we would go to collect piñons with our entire Navajo family. . . . Sometimes we made it a weekend excursion, cooking outdoors, kids running and playing together." Now memories such as these appear in Elizabeth's sculptures, which aren't meant to resemble specific people but do involve past experiences. Her delightful work demonstrates the imagination and artistry of the equally delightful artist.

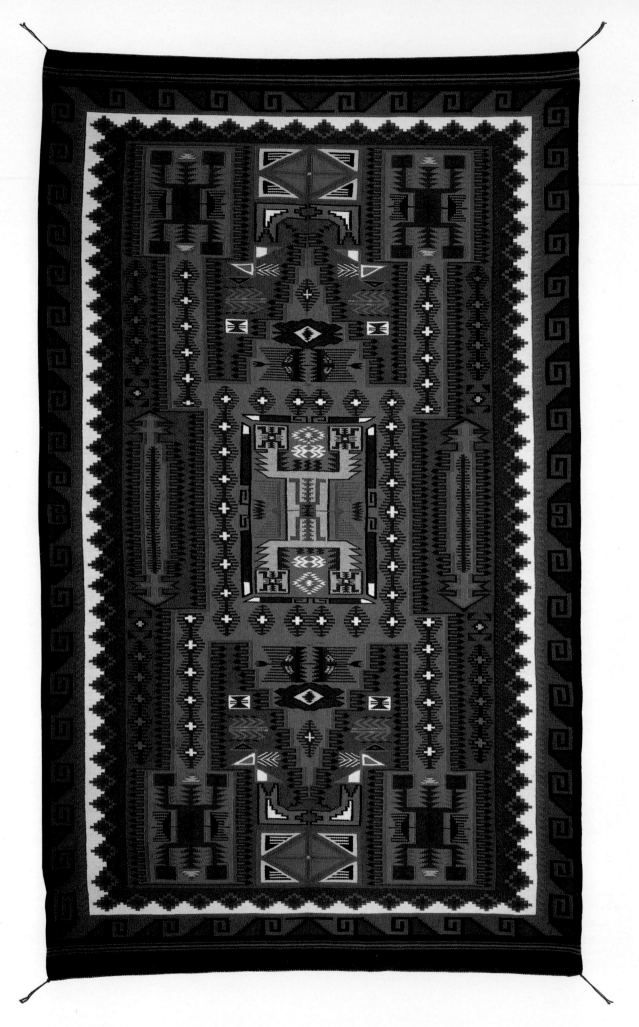

RIGHT: *This 18 1/2" tall sculpture was carved from cottonwood root by Navajo-Hopi artist Ambrose Teasyatwho. He says this piece is symbolic of both Talking God and the eagle that sacrifices its feathers for ceremonies.*

BELOW: *This striking 37 1/2" by 60" rug by Helen Kirk combines Teec Nos Pos designs with Ganado red colors.*

OPPOSITE: *Wanda Begody takes storm patterns to new heights in this complex 9 1/2' by 5 1/2' rug. The storm pattern is the only rug design (other than the pictorial) that is said to portray a natural event. The center rectangle, representing the Center of the Universe, is connected by "lightning paths" to the rectangles in each corner, which symbolize the four Sacred Mountains of Navajoland. Besides the large storm pattern in this rug, the center and corner rectangles also include miniature "storms."*

Tony Abeyta, unlike his sister Elizabeth, never considered any career but that of an artist. "I've always been a painter," Tony says. "There's never been any other choice. And I like the idea of being defined as a contemporary Indian painter. I've never been at rest with wanting to be an artist first who happens to be Indian. American Indians seem to have a very good sense of making order out of chaos, beauty out of confusion. I believe this contributes toward a prime motivating factor in the world of art. I try not to get lost in all that is part of this 'art world,' but to hold onto my ideas and beliefs."

Intermarriage between Navajo and Paiute peoples has had a strong influence on basketry. In fact, it is so common that in some instances it is almost impossible to detect tribal differences, and their basketry techniques and materials are identical.

Some artists cite influences such as art deco, Egyptian, and Scandinavian art, or classic icons: Michelangelo, Ansehm Keifer, Barbara Kruger, Rodin, Pia Castellani, Edgar Degas, Picasso. Others name more personal influences.

"I was beginning to be bored with my art," Wallace Begay said, "until I met a graduate student from Iran. She was so passionate about her art that I suddenly woke up again. She really impressed me with her enthusiasm, and it got me all fired up."

Rickie Nez spent time overseas in the military and, while there, "prowled European museums to study the masters." He says, "I absorbed the works of world-famous artists, and the appreciation of these masters inspired me to cultivate my talent."

Alvin Marshall took advantage of a similar opportunity, and visited Florence, Venice, and Milan. "I was fascinated by their art," he said. "I went to get more insight into art and art history. Instead I learned more about myself. I became detached from home and my normal environment. I was all alone and had time to think."

OPPOSITE: *Naveek (a name used to honor the Navajo-Greek heritage of the artist) creates unique and beautiful jewelry. Entitled* Children of Chaco, *this necklace was inspired by trips to Chaco Canyon with his grandfather, a* hataałi, *when Naveek was small. "As we sat among the ruins," Naveek said, "he would say, 'Listen. Listen. Listen to the spirits. There were once children just like you who played here. Now they are gone, but their spirits still live here. Listen to the spirits and never forget.' " The two 14-karat gold figures (the pendant) represent the children: lapis lazuli is the boy, Australian opal is the girl. The multiple strands of fresh water seed pearls are the Milky Way against the night sky of Chaco; the circles of lapis set in 14-karat gold are stars. The lapis clasp is Polaris, the guiding star. The companion bracelet (top),* Chaco Summer, *also contains lapis lazuli and Australian opal; the other bracelet,* Spring Blessing, *set with Australian opal and chrysoprase, was a gift for Naveek's daughter at birth.*

RIGHT, TOP AND BOTTOM: *Their mother's Pueblo ancestry shows in the work of brothers Michael and Andy Lee Kirk. Both draw upon Pueblo life for inspiration and both create stunning jewelry. A curved feather of 14-karat gold forms Michael Kirk's bracelet (top), which is set with a band of Australian opal. The feather-like features are formed by cutting and engraving the gold. Earrings are of sugilite and Australian opal set in 14-karat gold. Gold beads are combined with a kachina figure, which has a sand-cast gold tableta with cutout flute players. Stones include Mediterranean coral, lapis lazuli, opal, turquoise, and jet. The blue stone resembling turquoise in the face is gem silica. Pictured at bottom are 14-karat gold bracelets by Andy Lee Kirk. The lost wax casting method was used to create the bracelet (front) with three kachina faces; their eyes are set with (left to right) coral, turquoise, and an emerald-cut diamond. The other pieces are a combination of tufacast with some lost wax cast elements applied by the overlay technique. Settings include sugilite, pink and red coral, Australian opal, lapis lazuli, and turquoise. The bracelet in the foreground received First Prize at the 1991 Santa Fe Indian Market and Honorable Mention at the 1992 Heard Museum Indian Fair and Market. The bracelet at top received First Prize at the 1992 Santa Fe Indian Market.*

In 1978, Oreland Joe also traveled to Europe, not as an artist but as part of a group of hoop dancers. "We went to France," Oreland said, "but we did shows at night; I was free during the day. I absorbed the huge canvases and murals of the Louvre and the sculptures at Versailles. In 1986, I went back to Italy with a private company who takes students on working trips. Then I was selected as one of several U. S. artists to go to Japan to exhibit our work for nine days. When I visited the Metropolitan Museum in Tokyo, I never got out of the sculpture department."

Despite the importance of European artists, it is much more common for Navajos to name other Native American artists as their prime influence: T. C. Cannon, Helen Hardin, Allen Houser, Doug Hyde, Charlie Pratt, Bruce LaFountain, Marvin Toya, Otellie Loloma, Joseph Lonewolf, Charles Loloma, Charles Supplee, Roy Talahaftewa, Preston Monongye, White Buffalo, and Ted Charveze. Even more prominant are the names of contemporary, working Navajo artists: Jimmy Abeita, David Johns, Oreland Joe, Tim Washburn, Gibson Nez, James Little, Jake Livingston, Kenneth Begay, Harvey Begay, and Edison Smith.

"When I was just starting out, Oreland took time for me. . . . Now when younger artists come to see me, I try to help them all I can."—LARRY YAZZIE

Oreland Joe taught several sculptors the basics of his art, and influenced many more. Larry Yazzie speaks very highly of him.

"When I was just starting out," Larry said, "Oreland took time for me. None of the other sculptors would, and they wouldn't tell me how they accomplished certain things. Oreland was always willing to help and he was very humble. I saw how he was and thought I'd like to be like him. Now when younger artists come to see me, I try to help them all I can."

Museums around the country also help further the careers of fledgling artists. The Museum of Northern Arizona in Flagstaff, The Heard Museum in Phoenix, the Wheelwright Museum in Santa Fe, the Millicent Rogers Museum in Taos, the Southwest Museum in Los Angeles, the San Diego Museum of Man, and dozens of others concentrate on Native Americans and their art. Many schedule exhibitions in which ribbons and prize money are awarded, and this recognition and encouragement have great impact.

William Murphy resigned his position with the Navajo tribe in 1992 to become a full-time artist, but felt that things could be going better for him. Because he had entered the Gallup Ceremonial for several years without winning anything and was in need of funds, he considered selling the paintings he had planned to enter in the 1993 Gallup Ceremonial. However, his fourteen-year-old daughter encouraged him to keep one particular painting, saying that it was too good to sell and should be entered in the competition. William just made the deadline at Gallup, but the painting won a First Prize and Best of Category. Within a month, he had also won a poster contest in Farmington and an award

ABOVE: *Cheryl Marie Yestewa, Navajo-Hopi, is noted for her beadwork. Her infatuation with fine stones is evident in her work. "I'm a purist," she said. "I let the stones become the main focal point. I try to enhance the beauty of the material rather than overpower it." Cheryl works in both gold and silver, and all beads are shaped or rolled by hand. Materials in this jewelry (left to right) are white coral with lapis lazuli, turquoise with gold, and pink coral with sugilite.*

RIGHT: *This jewelry by Gibson Nez features gold overlay on silver with Lander's blue turquoise.*

at the New Mexico State Fair. His enthusiasm knew no bounds following his success.

The Gallup Intertribal Indian Ceremonial in New Mexico is only one of the organizations that offer special exhibitions. There is also New Mexico's Eight Northern Pueblos, O'Odham Tash in Casa Grande, Pueblo Grande Indian Market in Phoenix, as well as those that take place in communities on or near the reservation: Window Rock, Shiprock, Farmington, Chinle, and others. The Indian Arts and Crafts Association conducts trade fairs throughout the year for its members, and selects an Artist of the Year. The climax of the exhibition scene comes each August, when the Southwest Association of Indian Arts in Santa Fe hosts the largest "Indian Market" in the country. Most artists try to attend this extravaganza if no other.

"Before I'd left for Market, I had done some new designs and asked my dad to pray for them. He burned some cedar in the hogan and blew some smoke and prayed over my jewelry."—VICTOR BECK

OPPOSITE: *Jesse Monongye's inlay work makes him the undisputed master of lapidary. This multiple-exposure photograph shows multiple views of the butterfly and both sides of a reversible bear pendant on an exquisite necklace. The butterfly may be worn as a pin or attached to the elaborate gold link to become part of the necklace. The wings of the butterfly are hinged so they may be positioned to resemble flight.*

Victor Beck laughed as he related his first experience at the Santa Fe Indian Market. "In early 1975, I went to Market for the first time. I had done some really unique designs for that show. I got there on Friday just in time to enter my jewelry. There were probably no rooms to be had, but I don't think I had the money for one anyway. I parked by the La Fonda Hotel and slept in my car. I got to bed late and slept in the next morning until about 7:45 or so. When I woke up, I looked out and there were *all* these people all over the place. I went to pick up my jewelry and found out I'd won a bunch of First Prize awards. I finally got to my booth about 8:30, and there was a big crowd there. As I started putting my jewelry out, people were looking at it, grabbing pieces to try on, some were even writing checks. I didn't know what to do. I didn't even have all my work out yet. Someone from another booth saw my dilemma and came and helped me. By the time I finally got all set up, three-quarters of my jewelry was sold. Within an hour and a half, it was all gone. A woman came by and said, 'Oh, no, I wanted something of yours.' I threw both hands in the air and said, 'It's all gone.' She pointed to the ring on my finger and said, 'How about that piece?' I'd forgotten I even had it on. I took it off and she bought it. That night I got a room at the La Fonda. I just sat in a corner and counted the money over and over again.

"I called my mom and dad to tell them what had happened. Before I'd left for Market, I had done some new designs and asked my dad to pray for them. He burned some cedar in the hogan and blew some smoke and prayed over my jewelry. He said he had prayed for me all my life, but it was the first time he had prayed over my jewelry. He was very proud of me, and that made me happy because he was never really interested in art as a career for us. He felt that it was not worth doing. He was a member of the Tribal Council for twenty years, and he wanted us kids to be politicians, too."

Although it seems somewhat contradictory for parents to encourage children to excel at art but not to consider it as a career, that is just what many Navajo parents do. Art is simply a part of their tradition, something one does "on the side" for additional income. Their desire is to see well-educated children become doctors, lawyers, businessmen—or even politicians.

Victor Beck did become a member of the Navajo Tribal Council, representing the Piñon Chapter. "I gave twelve years of my life to tribal affairs," he said. "People were coming around from six o'clock in the morning on. I had no time to work on jewelry. I was in my prime and making money when I started. I left broke and with my artwork and tools gathering dust. Now I just want to get back to art."

Alfred Joe, a Tribal Council member from Dilcon, says he now only makes two or three pieces of jewelry a year. "The Tribal Council doesn't leave me a lot of time," he said. "Right now, I'm working on trying to get the tribe to create a place for artists to exhibit and sell their work. Many Navajos are very good artists, but know nothing about marketing."

Even with all the emphasis on art and artists in the Navajo community, artists are sometimes cautioned against excessive use of their talent. Virgil Nez explained, "My grandmother always said, 'Don't be painting so much. The Anasazi did it and they disappeared!' But I can't help it; I suppose I was born to paint."

"My grandmother always said, 'Don't be painting so much. The Anasazi did it and they disappeared!' But I can't help it; I suppose I was born to paint."—VIRGIL NEZ

When he was a youngster, Redwing Nez got much the same advice from a medicine man. "He told me not to draw," Redwing said. "He said 'only the Maker can draw. He makes everyone different. He is the artist. You're trying to imitate the deities.' You can see how much attention I paid to him." Redwing grinned as he looked around a studio cluttered with canvases in various stages of completion.

It is difficult to keep talented people from seeing everything from an artistic viewpoint. Even those who choose other careers often find themselves drawn back to art, and finally return to it full-time.

Almost without exception, the greatest influence mentioned by artists is memories: *I remember* . . . "my grandmother who was an herbalist"; "my grandfather who was a medicine man"; "my mother and grandmother weaving"; "herding sheep"; "being taught to respect the environment"; "drawing on cliffs"; "nature"; "the ceremonies"; "the legends"; "the stories"; "the past."

Memories may well be the strength of Navajo culture. In the *Diné* world, everything is interrelated and connected. As artists reach into the past for inspiration, they develop a better understanding of and appreciation for the culture that inspired them in the first place.

OPPOSITE: *Untitled sand texture and oil on canvas, 68" by 49", by Tony Abeyta, who is noted for his powerful portrayals of the Holy People.*

This unique Tiffany-style lamp was made by twenty-nine-year-old Allen Aragon. The lamp base and shade are high-fired clay with Pueblo pottery designs. A potter's wheel was used to make the lamp shade; the base was formed in a mold. Designs were painted on the clay prior to kiln firing. After firing, they were coated with a clear lead glaze and turquoise was added. The shade is decorated with silver rope chain and tubes accented with black onyx beads. A matching design is etched into the glass chimney.

"It is through my art," Beverly Blacksheep said, "that I've come to realize a deep appreciation for my heritage and the importance of preserving that heritage for generations to come."

"I was raised by my grandparents," Jack To'Baahe Gene said. "They taught me to see things, to observe. My grandmother was a weaver, my grandfather was a medicine man. While I was growing up, they were teaching me art with everything they did, I just didn't realize it. We traveled slowly since we rode horseback, and they would say, 'See, the trees and plants are moving. They are alive.' We'd look at the clouds and the mountains. Now my art is based on all those things, but clouds are not just clouds anymore. I'm going beyond what my grandparents taught me. I now strive for the soul of clouds and mountains. I'm going beyond the surface, and I want people to look beyond the surface to the soul of my art."

"It is through my art that I've come to realize a deep appreciation for my heritage and the importance of preserving that heritage for generations to come."—BEVERLY BLACKSHEEP

IT IS MORNING, THE TIME OF CHANGE. The world is changing, Navajo culture is changing, and the artists change continually due to artistic growth and maturity. The Beauty Walk continues, and, as memories of the past continue to inspire individuals, morning moves onward toward day.

DAY-SKY

In Beauty may I dwell

In Beauty may I walk

In Beauty may it rain on my young men

In Beauty may it rain on my young women

In Beauty may it rain on my chiefs

In Beauty may it rain on us

In Beauty may our corn grow

On the trail of pollen, may it rain

In Beauty before us, may it rain

In Beauty behind us, may it rain

In Beauty below us, may it rain

In Beauty above us, may it rain

In Beauty all around us, may it rain

In Beauty may I walk

—— from The Nightway

ABOVE: *This 28" by 24" sandpainting,* Female Feather Hat Corn Dancers, *by Nelson Lewis, represents the ceremonial gathering of corn pollen. A rainbow arches over a corn stalk with roots reaching into the earth (black), which contains seeds of multicolored corn. The terraced border is also done in sand. Nelson collects materials from New Mexico, Colorado, and several locations in Arizona for use in his unusual works.*

PREVIOUS PAGE: The Quiet Thunder, *22" by 28" acrylic on linen canvas by Clifford Brycelea.*

DAY-SKY

The sun hangs high in the midday sky, and all is still. The landscape stretches endlessly

toward a distant monolith that seems to shift and shimmer in the noonday heat.

A small lizard flicks from behind a boulder and skitters across the sand.

A hawk circles in a sky of the palest cornflower blue high above.

The color deepens to azure, then peacock, and finally to a deep, rich turquoise where the sky meets the purple mountains on the distant horizon.

Storm clouds begin to gather, and the rumble of thunder is heard in the distance. A breeze flirts with the tips of the juniper trees. The wind freshens as it is pushed before the rapidly approaching storm, and spirals of dust pirouette giddily across the landscape. Suddenly the sky darkens and lightning flashes. A cottontail runs for cover; sheep huddle together under juniper trees that dance in the wind. As the thunder crashes again and again, the heavens open and turbulent Male Rain pours down upon an eagerly awaiting Mother Earth.

Just as suddenly, it is over. The storm sweeps on, leaving behind the fragrance of rain-washed juniper and sage. The cottontail comes out of hiding; the lizard scales a nearby boulder. The gentle, misty Female Rain lingers in the distance, and a rainbow arches into the sky. The hawk soars above an earth that is refreshed and new.

The earth's growing cycle requires sunshine and rain, and Day-Sky, the South, is symbolic of summer, a time of fruitfulness. In the Navajo Walk, it is the time that represents youth and growth, a time to carry out the activities and pursue the goals set at Morning-Dawn.

In pursuit of these goals, some artists leave the reservation to attend universities or art schools; Larry Yazzie attended

IAIA, the school mentioned most often by Navajo artists. "I went there to study painting," he said, "but I was always interested in sculpture. I didn't see how anyone could carve stone, but I took the class. I was given studio space, stone, chisels, and a hammer and told to go for it." That teaching method apparently worked well for Larry. He is one of the most respected sculptors in today's Native American art world.

"IAIA is great," Patrick Smith agreed. "It brings different artists together and each has new ideas. I'd like to go on and get my master's in fine arts. We need more Native American professors teaching Native Americans."

Diné teaching *Diné* is exactly what the Navajo Community College is all about, yet all to often it is omitted from lists of influential schools. However, it is mentioned time and again by Navajo artists who learned their basic skills from excellent teachers there. This small college is responsible not only for stimulating an interest in art but also for instilling cultural pride.

Artists often go farther afield for additional training—to Arizona universities as well as those in other states, or to art schools in Chicago, Oakland, San Francisco. Victor Beck studied under a German silversmith at an upstate New York

Forefathers, *a 60" by 72" oil on canvas, is the work of Jeanette Katoney, who said, "When I painted this, my thoughts were at one with 'the Ancient Ones,' the Anasazi. The spiral represents two worlds: our prior existence and our life now. The figures symbolize First Woman and First Man as human beings; they gave us life and intelligence."*

university. "He taught me to do a 'clean job,'" Victor said. "Any bit of solder on your work and it came back to you. I learned to use simplicity in design. He would tell us just to take one or two lines and try to create something."

Fortunately, many of these schools seem to have recognized the talent of these Native Americans and allowed it to follow its own course. Nelson Tsosie attended the University of Arizona, where his major required a class in two-dimensional design.

"It was all abstract," Nelson said. "They would give us a piece of wire or a bar of soap and say 'make something.' I was a painter, but that taught me to see design in third-dimensional form. I changed my major to fine arts."

Some artists return home after a taste of living in "that other world," some stay in urban areas. Some are comfortable moving back and forth between two worlds, some are not.

This gold jewelry by twenty-nine-year-old Vernon A. Begaye is set with red and pink coral, turquoise, lapis lazuli, sugilite, opal, and jet. The bola tie and each concho of the silver belt have four bears moving clockwise or sunwise, the direction that is ceremonially correct among the Diné.

Andersen Kee obtained an associate degree in art at IAIA, but then dropped out of Oakland's California College of Arts and Crafts after one year. "The school was excellent," he explained. "They had small classes, lots of personal attention. But I just couldn't handle the city." Back home, he decided to try to earn a living with his art. "I remember thinking: this is what I went to school for, I might as well give it a shot." He is a gifted artist, and his oil portraits of historic figures are very powerful. One wonders if that strength would have developed if Andersen had stayed away from his homeland.

"I couldn't last two weeks in L.A. I went as a kid and thought it was wonderful to see everything and watch the TV, but it wasn't like being among these rocks. I can spend an hour just looking at one rock."—REDWING NEZ

Redwing Nez laughed when "city life" was mentioned. "I couldn't last two weeks in L.A.," he said. "I went as a kid and thought it was wonderful to see everything and watch the TV, but it wasn't like being among these rocks. I can spend an hour just looking at one rock."

Baje Whitethorne also shared his feelings about living in that "other world." "Sometimes we go where the grass is greener only to find that the signs all say 'Keep off the grass.' We go back home where we feel secure. We want to give something of our culture to our kids and make sure they're well taught. If we deny them this, what have they gained? Keeping up with the Joneses is not the most important thing."

SOME ARTISTS WORK SOLELY TOWARD the goal of becoming an artist; others consider their art an avocation and plan different careers only to have fate take a hand.

"I didn't get into jewelry until 1968," Lee Yazzie said. "I had hip surgery, and when I got out of the hospital, I had to have something to do. My parents were traditional silversmiths, so I learned metal work from them. I learned lapidary more-or-less on my own, and I did some inlay for Preston [Monongye] for a while. When I started, the Zunis were doing most of the inlay; I wanted to do something different, so I learned."

"Sometimes we go where the grass is greener only to find that the signs all say 'Keep off the grass.' "—BAJE WHITETHORNE

Herbert Taylor, who has been a full-time jeweler since 1984, creates spectacular gold and silver jewelry using only the finest grade of turquoise and other stones. For fifteen years he was a welder who made jewelry simply as a sideline. "Then one day," he said, "I made a silver bracelet with five pieces of Persian turquoise in it—and traded it for a set of tires. Believe me, I needed those tires, but I said to myself, 'This is where the money is.' What's more, I'm still doing the same thing I did as a welder, only on a smaller scale."

Some artists depend on their art for a livelihood, others must find employment to augment their art income. Life can be a struggle, particularly for younger artists who have yet to receive public recognition. Most of them have families and many are employed full-time in non–art-related occupations. However, art supports many Navajos as they attend colleges, universities, or art schools.

Ray Scott, age twenty-seven, sold his jewelry as a means of support while earning his degree from the University of Arizona, with majors in both finance and business administration. Although he received a scholarship and has been accepted into Berkeley's University of California School of Law, he has put those plans on hold in order to see just where his artistic talents may lead.

Leslie Pablo, twenty-eight, on the other hand, took up sculpting because of a lack of employment in Albuquerque where he and his family were living while his wife attended school. "I tried making one small sculpture, and sold it the day I finished it. That really encouraged me. Then when we moved to Farmington, I discovered sculptor Tim Washburn living right across the street. He taught me what's important in sculpture and helped me work on proportion."

OPPOSITE: Horse's Ghost, *an 18 1/2" tall alabaster sculpture by twenty-eight-year-old Cindy Fowler Penn.*

"He taught us to discipline ourselves, and to always try to do our best on each piece of art we produced."—CINDY PENN

BELOW: *Alabaster sculptures by twenty-seven-year-old Cheryl A. Joe. At right is Walks With Anger, 7" tall and 7 1/2" long; at left is an untitled piece 4 3/4" tall.*

OPPOSITE: *This New Lands style rug was woven by twenty-three-year-old Patricia Watson Tsinnie. The 32" by 65" rug combines a raised outline technique with Burntwater colors and a Teec Nos Pos design.*

Both Cindy Penn, twenty-nine, and Cheryl Joe, twenty-seven, credit sculptor Oreland Joe with introducing them to sculpture in a Shiprock High School art class, and encouraging them to continue. "Oreland taught us some of the basics of the 'art business,'" Cindy explained, "such as advertising and marketing and how to present ourselves and our work. He taught us to discipline ourselves, and to always try to do our best on each piece of art we produced."

There are a multitude of Navajo artists in their twenties. Some have begun to make a name for themselves, others are just getting started, but there is a wealth of new talent on the rise. Some of these younger artists are already beginning to "put something back" into their culture. Peter Ray James, twenty-nine, works with American Indian students, primarily at reservation schools, through the Arts in Education Program funded by the State of New Mexico. "I enjoy working with students and want to encourage them," Peter said. "I'd also like to see more Indian artists helping these kids. Of one hundred artists in this program, only two of us are Native Americans."

Bob Lansing's contemporary pottery is non-traditional in every way; his pots are thrown on a wheel and fired in a kiln. Influenced by the work of the renowned potter Joseph Lonewolf, he carves and incises animal motifs and designs of Navajo and Pueblo origin into these works of art. The piece shown here is 10 1/2" in diameter.

Harold Davidson, twenty-nine, demonstrates his sculpting techniques at Navajo schools and talks to students about drugs and alcohol as well as art. Harold, who is a recovering alcoholic, says, "It's great to talk to the kids. They know I've been there, so I know what I'm talking about. You can see the frustration on their faces. But I talk about myself and my problems with alcohol, and tell them that if they really want something, they just have to work for it. We talk about everything, and find that we often share the same ideas. We sometimes talk for hours. By the time it's over, their attitudes have changed; they want

Silver jewelry by twenty-six-year-old Ray Scott. The designs in the bracelet and belt were made by the overlay technique with granulated backgrounds. The silver beads were "shaved" in a ball-bearing machine, which results in the satin finish.

to come talk to me personally. It makes me feel good when I see one of them later and they're doing well; they've changed."

Navajo youths are often frustrated and confused by the inconsistencies of the two worlds in which they find themselves. Self-esteem is further diminished by unfortunate circumstances at times. In the past, for example, names were changed arbitrarily with no thought given to how an individual might feel about losing his or her identity.

Ray Scott explained a change in surname that occurred during the Korean conflict. "Our Navajo name was Taa'itsohii (Morning Gold), but no one could pronounce it," Ray said. "My father's mail was sent to 'Raymond, in care of Scott' (his captain). By the time my father returned home, he had become Ray Scott, as I am now. However, we're taking steps to have our name changed back to the original."

Baje Whitethorne feels that "people still know nothing about Indians. They think we're all running around in feathered headdresses and breechcloths. Once I was a guest at a reception at the Museum of Natural History in New York. I heard people talking, wondering when 'the Indian' was going to get there. I was standing right there, but they were looking for someone a little more exciting, I guess."

Redwing Nez laughed and shook his head when he spoke of the New York gallery owner who told him that he "would sell a lot more paintings if he would just wear a war bonnet." That attitude in this day and age is surprising but, unfortunately, it still exists.

However, Day-Sky is a time of growth and fruitfulness and, for every negative-image story of the Navajo, there is a matching success story about an artist who struggled and won. Redwing Nez also spoke of his early years as a struggling artist.

"I wondered sometimes just what I was doing. I walked away from the university, walked away from a paying job, to lose my mind in painting. Those were

Redwing Nez laughed and shook his head when he spoke of the New York gallery owner who told him that he "would sell a lot more paintings if he would just wear a war bonnet."

back in the starving days. My buddy and I lived on hotdogs, popcorn, and instant tea. We drooled over the steaks on TV and went to artists' receptions to eat. We used to joke about who was going to give up first and go live off the government. But I wasn't about to. There were times when I struggled, but I had to make it or just give up and throw the paints away. We made it. My wife and I have never gone on the dole."

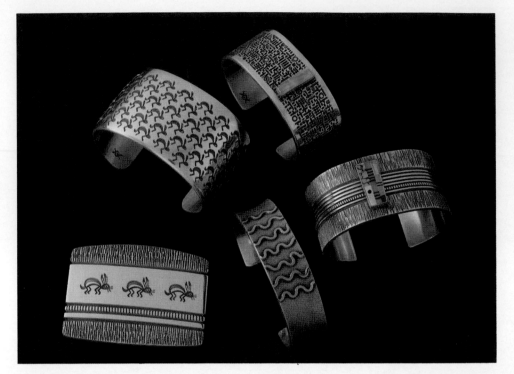

ABOVE: *Noted for his unusual contemporary jewelry, Norbert Peshlakai combines stamping, carving, engraving, and filing in his work. His stamps are handmade from concrete nails, and he continually adds to his collection. Adapted from an ancient Mimbres pottery design, the rabbits on the belt buckle required the use of nine different stamps. The 14-karat gold designs on the lower bracelet were appliquéd. Settings include opal (top right) and, at far right, a mosaic of pink coral, opal, turquoise, lapis lazuli, jet, and fossilized walrus ivory.*

OPPOSITE: *Jack To'Baahe Gene's 24 1/2" by 18 1/2" pastel and sand is titled Nature/Herbalist Impassioned. The artist noted that "the trees are like a cathedral of nature. The Navajo lady is an herbalist; she harmonizes with nature. Everything around her responds—they become part of her, she becomes part of them. To my forefathers, everything was looked upon as powerful—the trees, the plants, the mountains."*

Robert Taylor recalled a like incident. "I remember, back in 1986, I was in construction and times were tough. I got laid off and I didn't even get my last paycheck. I looked for work, but there just weren't any jobs to be had in construction. Finally we ran out of money and food. Cheryl [a daughter] was only about two and she was hungry. We had one box of macaroni and cheese that Christine fixed." Robert could laugh about it now. "I'll never forget eating that macaroni and cheese. Christine's folks happened to come by and they went and bought us some groceries. When I finally got my check, I bought some silver. I made a necklace and took it to Byron Hunter at The Heard Museum gift shop. Tripled my money. I said 'To heck with construction,' and I never went back."

Fidel Bahe has been making jewelry for years, but as a result of an accident in 1993, he lost the sight in one eye for a time. Something he didn't realize when he was casting jewelry during that time is that one needs both eyes for proper perspective. When his eyesight was finally restored, he discovered that he had been adding an extra level to his castings. Deciding that he liked it that way, he is now experimenting with three levels instead of the traditional two in his tufacast jewelry.

"My accident was financially devastating," Fidel said, "but it was spiritually, emotionally, and creatively rewarding. It not only showed me a new design, but just how precious life is."

Jesse Monongye's struggle was of another kind, but he too won his battle. Although he was producing spectacular jewelry in the early 1980s, Jesse's life was a disaster due to drug and alcohol addiction. "I finally hit bottom in 1984," Jesse said. "That's when I gave up and went for treatment; I've been clean ever since. I had to learn the hard way, but it made me a better man." Jesse is now married and lives with his wife and a "yours, mine, and ours" family of six children in Scottsdale, Arizona, where he continues to create superb masterpieces.

Jesse is also raising funds for an organization called Shánídíín. The word refers to the first rays of morning light streaking upward from behind the clouds. Here, it represents the "beginning of a new life." Jesse's plans include a civic center with a gym and drug/alchohol counseling office on the Navajo Reservation; the search is underway for land on which to build. "We have to learn to better ourselves through teaching," he said, "teaching the people to help themselves." He hopes that by working through the children, he can also encourage Native Americans to seek autonomy.

ABOVE: *The pottery of Jimmy and Clara Wilson resembles older Navajo wares, yet the shapes are often non-traditional, such as the cup and the tall vase at right. Traditional designs—yei'iis, corn, and geometrics—are incised and appliquéd on their work, and it is covered with pitch, as is most Navajo pottery.*

RIGHT: *This large wedding vase (21" tall) was made by Betty Manygoats. Due to the significance of horned toads in Navajo lore and legend, their likeness is often included in pottery. Noted artist Shonto Begay explains in his book* Ma'ii and Cousin Horned Toad, *"Whenever we come upon a horned toad, we gently place it over our heart and greet it 'Ya ateeh shi che'' ('Hello, my grandfather'). We believe it gives strength of heart and mind. We never harm our grandfather."*

Butterfly designs have become popular among Navajo and Ute basketmakers. The colorful pictorial baskets by Grace Lehi (top) and her niece, Rose Ann Whiskers (center), are 12 1/2" and 11" in diameter. Sally Black combined petroglyphic figures (more common in baskets of the Apache, Pima, and Tohono O'Odham) and butterfly designs in the elaborate 25 1/2" diameter coiled basketry plaque (below). It was awarded First Prize at the 1993 Gallup Intertribal Indian Ceremonial.

The design of this 54" by 33" weaving by Bruce T. and Nadine Nez is commonly referred to as a Tree of Life. It features a corn stalk growing from a basket and eighty-nine different birds.

Teddy Draper Jr. took his last drink in 1983, but continues to battle the ongoing war against alcohol and drugs by devoting his time and efforts to the Chinle, Arizona, Youth Athletic Club. "We supervise sports and other activities," Teddy explained. "A Player of the Month is chosen, not based on points made in games, but on good grades, attendance, and attitude. We're trying to build self-esteem in these kids. And no drinking or drug use is allowed—by the coaches or the kids." Teddy not only works with youngsters, but is a talented artist who owns a gallery near Canyon de Chelly, is on the Board of Directors of the Gallup Intertribal Indian Ceremonial, and is in charge of the Fine Arts Exhibition at the Navajo Nation Fair in Window Rock.

Joe Ben Jr. called from Paris, where he was teaching a class at the *École de Beaux Art*. "My father always told me to know where you came from, know who you are, and know where you are going. During my college years, I took some time to pull back and ask myself those questions. Now I have this concept of who I am; as a Navajo, I am as good as anyone else and they are as good as me. We're all equal. I not only can express myself with my art, but as an artist I can say where I want to live; I can even teach in a prestigious art school such as this. I am a Navajo, but I am also an artist, a teacher, a human being. I live and function just as every-one else does. That is the strength of art."

That art, in turn, is strengthened by the artists' love of their Navajo homeland. There, among the mountains and canyons of their youth, they absorb the beauty of the landscape, or sit in that special silence that seems to calm the soul, or live an orderly life in harmony with man and nature. The Navajos hold nature in awe, believing that it is the master of man, rather than the reverse. They accept whatever it brings, and offerings are made and prayers said to appease its forces.

"I am a Navajo, but I am also an artist, a teacher, a human being. I live and function just as everyone else does. That is the strength of art."—JOE BEN JR.

"In my youth I learned to see the world about me," Shonto Begay said, "to savor the beauty and to feel at home among the red mesas, piñon, and juniper. My world was the circular line of the horizon. This was the place that harbored the ancient gods and animal beings that were so alive in the stories of my people. The teachings of my elders made it very clear that this land is sacred and we belong to it; it does not belong to us. I learned that nature was more than just

ABOVE: *The sandpainting by Johnny Benally Sr. entitled* Whirling Logs with Storm *combines elements of nature with ceremonial designs—yei'iis, feathers, and sacred plants (clockwise from top left: corn, tobacco, beans, and squash). The center of the design represents water, with a sun face in each of the Four Directions. The small white designs extending outward from the center are the roots of the Four Sacred Plants. Also shown are the Four Sacred Mountains (top), four pairs of birds, and the night sky. "My great-grandfather was a medicine man," Johnny said, "and I was brought up with all this. I've always been fascinated by sandpaintings."*

RIGHT: *This unusual 29" diameter basket by Elsie Holiday combines a turtle design with a positive-negative reverse pattern in the center.*

ABOVE: *Robert Becenti portrays a familiar scene from the not-so-distant past of the Navajos in this 16" by 32" oil on canvas, Cross Roads.*

OPPOSITE: *My Mother's Kitchen, a 54" by 40" acrylic on canvas by Shonto Begay, won First Prize at the 1993 Santa Fe Indian Market. "My works are personal visions shared, and the series of small brush strokes repeat like the words of Blessingway prayers. For me, the process is a visual chant."*

what I saw . . . she gives and maintains life. She commands humility and respect."

Navajo artists show their appreciation of nature by including various apects of it in their art. Simple pottery styles are often adorned with appliquéd designs of corn, lizards, or horned toads. Most Navajo pottery is sparsely decorated, possibly due to the taboo against making painted pottery except for special ceremonial purposes.

A 1993 Navajo pottery exhibition at the Arizona State Museum included a quote from Mae Adson Shonto on this issue in an exhibit caption. "The Anasazi started to over-decorate their pottery and the Wind destroyed them because of that. That is why to this day we are told not to decorate pottery."

Jimmy and Clara Wilson explained the intricacies of the pottery-making process. "We learned from my cousin, Faye Tso," Jimmy said. "She learned from her grandmother and great-grandmother; it's been passed along for years.

"I learned that nature was more than just what I saw . . . she gives and maintains life. She commands humility and respect."— SHONTO BEGAY

"We get clay from places like Black Mesa and Sunset Crater. It is really hard. Some is down very deep and we have to dig it up. That is our tradition. A man came to us one time to buy pottery and told us some people use old pottery for temper and that's what we should do. But the medicine men don't want us to use old pottery. It belongs to the Anasazi."

"When we were kids," Clara added, "our mothers told us never to pick up those potteries. 'Don't touch,' they said. 'They belong to the Anasazi. They are for the dead. Leave those spirits alone.' So we don't use those old pots, we use our own clays."

"We mix several clays together," Jimmy explained, "then make long coils and build up the pot. Then we dry it and smooth it out with a corn cob. Designs are etched in or appliquéd, but you can't close the design."

"It should be open someplace," Clara added. "There are all these things in your mind, so there has to be an open space so your mind can go in and out and your design can go with you."

"We fire with juniper wood in a pit," Jimmy went on. "We pile wood on until it gets red hot and glows like hot iron. It takes six hours or more to get the pots really hard; it takes a lot of wood. We let the pots cool overnight, then clean the ashes off and wash them."

"In the summer, we take all the kids and go into the forest to pick pitch," Clara said. "It's a hard job. Sometimes the kids climb up into the trees to get it. But we have to check the trees to see if there's been a lightning strike. Even if there's lots of pitch there, if there's been a lightning strike, we don't bother that one. Faye is a medicine woman and she's very strict about those rules. 'Don't

Ancient and Modern Art, *a 24" by 20" watercolor by Harrison Begay (Haskey Yahne Yah). In this scene, young Navajo shepherds sketch charcoal drawings on a cliff face already marked with prehistoric Anasazi "art." Charcoal drawings that record events of the past century may be seen in Canyon de Chelly National Monument.*

ABOVE: Shepherdess, *22" by 30" watercol-or by Robert Draper.*

RIGHT: Spiritual Transformation, *a 23" by 17 1/2" acrylic on canvas board by Wayne Beyale, won Second Prize at the 1993 Gallup Intertribal Indian Ceremonial.*

ABOVE: *Although Thomas Singer's work has the massive look of traditional Navajo jewelry of the 1940s and '50s, his unique styling places it in a class of its own. These pieces are set with turquoise and variscite (green).*

OPPOSITE: *Twenty-five-year-old Charles Morris learned the overlay technique and began adding wildlife designs to his jewelry when his father suggested he transfer his painting skills to silver. His work is more delicate and detailed than most over-* *lay. Designs cut from one sheet of silver are soldered onto another, the silver is oxidized to darken it, then buffed and polished, leaving only the lower layer black. Satin finishes are accomplished with fine sandpaper. The necklace is set with lapis lazuli.*

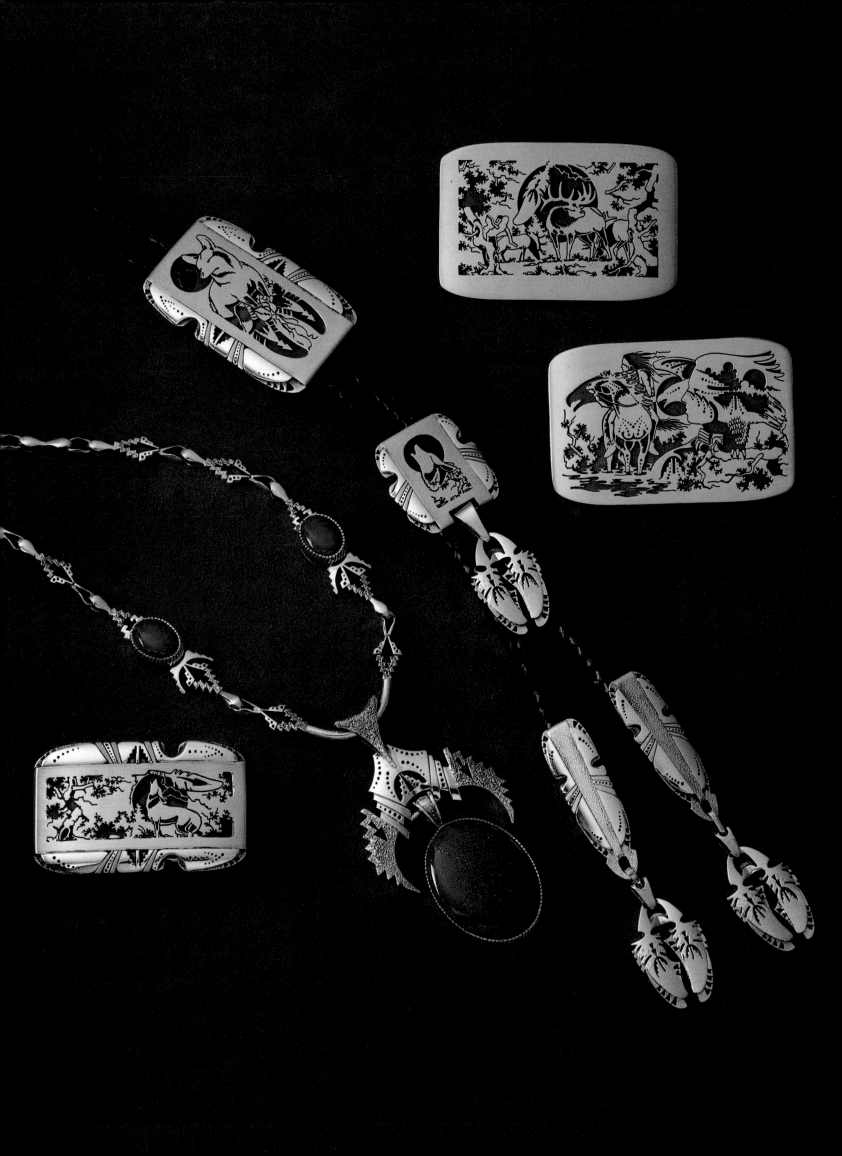

bother those trees with lightning strikes,' she says. 'Find a good one.' We take Vaseline or lard along to get the pitch off our hands.

"We heat the pitch to a liquid and strain it so it's nice and clean. We make swabs by wrapping an old sock around the end of a stick, then covering that real tight with strips of old sheets and string. We make all sizes: big ones for the big pots, tiny ones for the miniatures. The pots are warmed, ready to glaze. Everything has to be ready because it all has to be done fast. We put the pots on wax paper and swab on the hot pitch, then we rub the pots with balls of wax paper to make them shine, then set them on more wax paper to dry."

Although much of today's Navajo pottery is sparsely decorated, a few potters are branching out into new areas. Bob Lansing's work is thrown on a wheel and fired in a kiln. Carved, incised, and painted designs include geometric shapes, symbolism, and wildlife—feathers and butterflies, eagles and bears.

"I saw some of Joseph Lonewolf's pottery, and I thought maybe I could do that," Bob explained. "I learned the basics of decorating the pottery from William Yazzie, but I was working on greenware [commercially mass-produced pottery] and different people kept telling me I should make my own. Finally Lawrence Crank taught me to throw pots on a wheel. Most potters used geometrics, so I wanted to do something different. I decided on wildlife. The bear is my Navajo brother; the feathers are guardians for protection."

The Wanderers, a 20" by 15" watercolor by Ernest Franklin Sr., was awarded First Prize at the 1993 Gallup Intertribal Indian Ceremonial.

"We walk in sacredness with the Great Spirit. He gives us everything on earth, and everything is here for a reason. We are not just to see the beauty, but see what nature has to teach."—ALVIN MARSHALL

Baskets are also a popular medium for displays of nature's bounty. The oldest Navajo craft art, basketmaking has been one of the least practiced, but some exemplary basketmakers are now staging a comeback. They weave award-winning baskets with geometric and ceremonial designs as well as birds, butterflies, and animals.

ABOVE: *Contemporary Ganado red style rug, 41" by 55", by Freda Manymules. Ganado rugs typically have a red background, with white, black, and gray designs inside a black border. A central figure—often a diamond or two—is surrounded by serrates, crosses, zigzags, and other geometric shapes.*

RIGHT: *Navajo rug designs are inlaid into the jewelry of Robert B. Henry Jr. The bracelet is inlaid with jet, tuquoise, and sugilite; the bola with tuquoise, jet, spiney oyster shell, and mother-of-pearl. In these two pieces of jewelry, 881 individual stones were used along with 846 silver strips that form the channels; there are fifty-six small sun faces on the bola tie. Both pieces received First Prize at the 1993 Gallup Intertribal Indian Ceremonial. "The idea of doing rugs came from my grandmother," Robert said. "She taught me to set up her loom when I was small. Now I am a silver rug weaver."*

ABOVE: *An exceptional Klagetoh style weaving, 69" by 54 1/2", by Alice Begay. Although there is an abundance of red in this rug, as there is in Ganados, the predominant gray background more accurately places it in the Klagetoh category.*

OPPOSITE: *Vernon C. Haskie made this overlay bola tie set with Morenci tuquoise and the extraordinary concho belt that has a different rug design on each of ten conchos. He was awarded a First Prize for the bola tie and a Second Prize for the concho belt at the 1993 Gallup Intertribal Indian Ceremonial.*

OPPOSITE AND BELOW: *This elaborate silver box by Clarence Lee has won awards throughout the Southwest. Memories of Clarence's traditional Navajo lifestyle unfold in designs both inside and out: horses, dogs, and sheep; a weaver; a tire swing; pickup trucks and horse trailer; helicopter and airplane flying overhead; mountains; the windmill with the number "14" (the number of the well from which his family hauled water); the watering trough with water made of turquoise; the dog "lifting a leg" at the foot of the windmill tower; and much more. Because his parents met at a squaw dance, Monument Valley became the setting of just such a scene on the bottom of the box (inset, opposite). The underside of the lid (below) is adorned with butterflies, bees, ladybugs, dragonflies, a hummingbird, and other insects set with various stones.*

"We walk in sacredness with the Great Spirit," Alvin Marshall said. "He gives us everything on earth, and everything is here for a reason. We are not just to see the beauty, but see what nature has to teach."

"In our Navajo mythology," Peter Ray James explained, "it is said that we passed through different worlds with all sorts of insects, animals, plants, medicine, and spiritual beings. My cultural philosophy is a creation of power with color as a foundation to knowledge, prayers, medicine, and understanding. I feel that I am in this circle of spirituality and as long as my way of life is in the rainbow of my traditional values, I am blessed with Beauty."

The lifestyle may have changed over the years, but the basic tenets of the Navajo Way have not. The Trail of Beauty still leads to a long life and many still keep the traditions.

Andersen Kee says, "Certain things will always be there—the way of thinking and the beliefs. Tradition is still passed on through example and oral history."

As the outside world continues to close in, there are those—though their numbers are fewer—who still speak the language, live in hogans, and tend the sheep much as they did in the early days. Holding onto their culture, their values, and their land is a way of surviving, but as the tribe has increased in numbers, the land cannot possibly support all of them in the traditional way.

As Joe Ben Jr. says, "Cultures need to evolve and grow. Look at the European cultures. Their difficulties evolved into something new. Our culture is not the same now as it was a hundred years ago. It is evolving. That's what keeps it alive."

The Navajo Way stresses stability and harmony by submersion in family: patience, sharing, cooperating, and controlling excessive desires. The outside world, on the other hand, screams that it's every man for himself: "Try to get ahead, you must be somebody!" Navajo artists often find themselves torn between two worlds.

The problem, in fact, can go much deeper for those who were raised in urban environments. Harvey Begay talked very candidly about it. "I was the only or the first Navajo to do most of the things I've done in my life," he said.

"At the time, I was the only Navajo attending Scottsdale High School and later ASU, the only one in my Navy squadron and, although I can't be sure, as far as I know I was the only Navajo flier in Vietnam. I know I was the only Navajo flier at McDonnell-Douglas later, and I'm the only Navajo in our neighborhood now. People talk about Navajos living in two worlds, but when you've lived with Anglos in large cities most of your life, it puts you in some sort of 'no man's land'—not feeling totally accepted in either place."

Tim Washburn was adopted (along with his three sisters) by an Anglo family when his parents died. Only eight at the time, Tim spoke no English, had never tasted a hamburger, but he adjusted to the Anglo world. However, he remembered these early years and, once grown, moved his family back to Navajo country.

Even when early memories are basically the same, each artist presents them differently. Both Mark Silversmith and Conrad House cite memories as their motivation and, in one instance, both were further inspired by snow-capped Mt. Hesperus in the La Plata Mountains of Colorado. Yet their respective artwork has no resemblance.

"I thought of my grandparents and their grandparents before them and on and on. I thought of the natural beauty of the land and our relationship to it—our relationship to all life forms, even the sky, the night sky, and the Milky Way."— CONRAD HOUSE

Conrad interpreted the past in a colorful, complex montage of images entitled *Dibé Nitsaa,* or Big Sheep Mountain (Mt. Hesperus, the Sacred Mountain to the North). "I thought of my grandparents," he said, "and their grandparents before them and on and on. I thought of the natural beauty of the land and our

ABOVE AND OPPOSITE: *Both Mark C. Silversmith and Conrad House said their inspiration came from reflecting on the past and from viewing the snow-capped peaks of Colorado's La Plata Mountains; yet their emotions are expressed differently and their artwork bears no resemblence. The central figure in Conrad House's 30" by 22" pastel entitled* Dibé Nitsaa *(Big Sheep Mountain)* (above) *includes Conrad's hand with a cattail as the middle finger and the snow-capped mountains of Sisnajinni, the Sacred Mountain to the East. Also included are clouds that connect Mother Earth and Father Sky, a dragonfly to symbolize his grandmother, snakes to represent danger, Big Sheep Mountain (lower section), a heart, a turtle to symbolize his father's Oneida clan, a salmon to represent time spent in the Northwest, and many other aspects of nature. Mark C. Silversmith says of his 22" by 30" watercolor,* Ancient Echoes *(opposite), "I think of the peace Indians must have felt a long time ago, tracking through the quiet snow. I get most of my mountain landscapes from right outside my window. The La Plata Mountains to the north are snow-capped even in August."*

Distraction, *a 12 1/2" tall bronze by Nelson Tsosie. The tree stump and the ground were originally formed from clay, the rest from wax. The colors are a combination of conventional bronze patinas and acrylics. The squash blossom necklace is silver. This sculpture won Best of Category in the Indian Arts and Crafts Association's Artist of the Year competition for 1994.*

relationship to it—our relationship to all life forms, even the sky, the night sky, and the Milky Way. Everything is interrelated and interconnected and interdependent."

Mark Silversmith, on the other hand, portrayed a peaceful scene set in an quiet, snowy countryside. "I try to convey in my paintings what the mid-1800s Indian saw and felt," Mark explained. "Before reservation life, they could be themselves, in their own environment, living a nomadic life."

One reason the lifestyle is so prominant in Navajo art is that some art mediums are simply part of the *Diné* culture. As Mary Taylor said, "We just work at this. It's what we grew up with. Then people come along and say it's art."

"My mother was a weaver," Andersen Kee said. "My father did silverwork and painted. He did everyday life scenes. I didn't think much about it; I was just a kid. But I guess that's where I got my first ideas about wanting to paint."

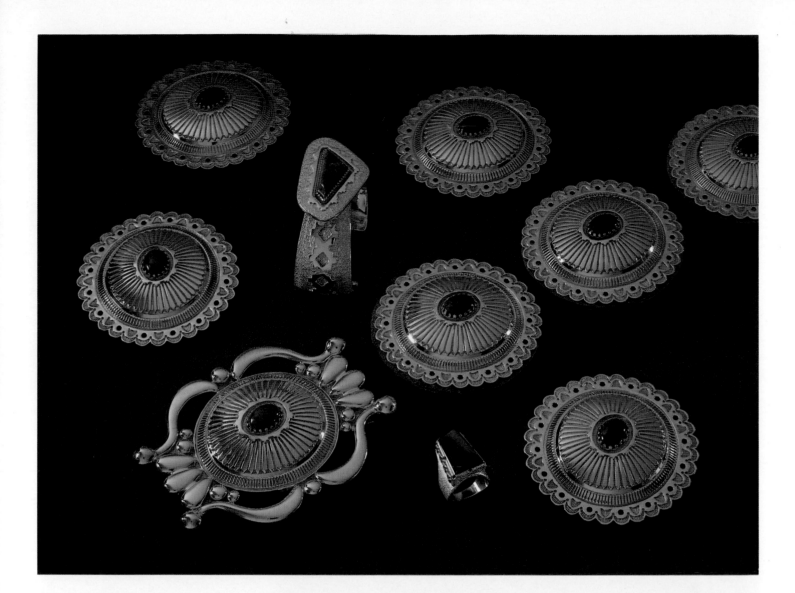

ABOVE: *Silverwork set with sugilite by Allison Lee ("Snowhawk"). The conchos were all hammered and stamped, the outer part of the buckle was cast. Both overlay and fused metal (granulation) techniques were used in making the ring and bracelet.*

RIGHT: *Silver jewelry by Steven J. Begay combines traditional designs with a contemporary jewelry style.*

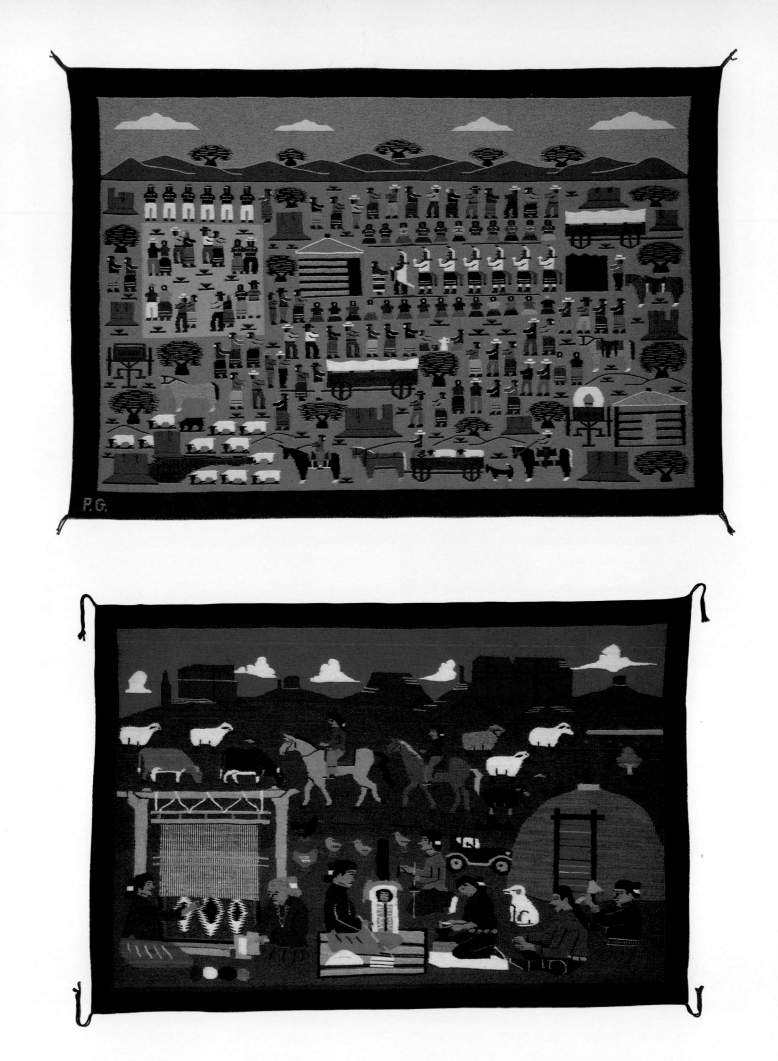

ABOVE AND OPPOSITE: *Pictorial weavings have long been favorites among both collectors and weavers. Various aspects of Navajo life are shown in these iconographies. Woven by a grandmother and granddaughter, Laura* *and Loretta Nez, the 34" by 41 1/2" rug pictured above portrays a trading post scene. The complex 48" by 70" pictorial weaving by Pauline Glasses (opposite, top) illustrates several traditional events, including a squaw* *dance (left in light area) and a yei'ii ceremony (center). The 33" by 49" pictorial rug by Betty Patterson (opposite, bottom) represents a scene in Monument Valley.*

Through the years, there have been few families that didn't include a silver-smith and even fewer without a weaver at the loom. Many artists joke about being sheepherders, but there is more there than meets the eye. With sheep herding came responsibility and the sense of unity so necessary to the Navajo family. There was also something inspiring about that time spent alone out under the open sky; artists mention those solitary hours time and again.

Harold Davidson says he spent the hours alone sketching—and daydreaming. "I used to dream of being a rodeo rider, and would think of the things I wanted to have when I grew up. I think those daydreams helped me pull myself out of some tough situations. Even when I was drinking, I didn't forget my dreams. I remembered the things I wanted—to have a better life and to be somebody. I think that's one thing that helped me stop. Now I ride saddle broncs in rodeos, and I'm very grateful for my art. It's good to know that some part of the dreams I had sitting on the mountain came true."

Others were also influenced by living the outdoor life and working with livestock. Rodeoing is the number-one sport on the reservation today, and several artists participate. Alvin Begay is somewhat reticient when discussing jewelry making, but loosens up when rodeo is mentioned. "My first love is bareback

Break A Wild Horse, an 18" by 24" oil on canvas by Robert Becenti.

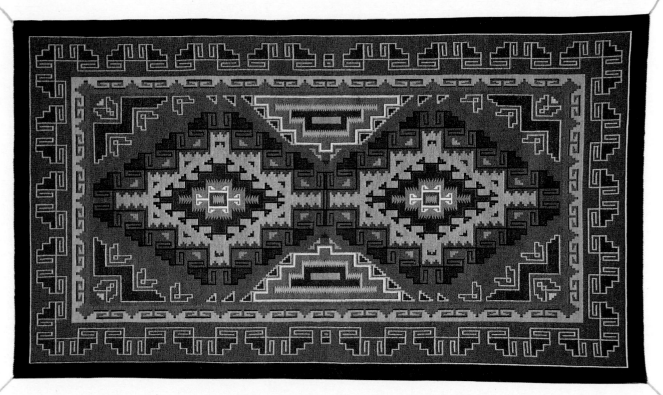

A 56 1/2" by 99" Two Grey Hills style rug by Rita Bedah. Two Grey Hills rugs are woven of natural, undyed wool in black, white, and brown. Blending different colors of wool results in the variety of subtle shades.

riding," he said. "I've been competing for twenty years, and I qualified for the Indian National Finals several years." His wife Lula added the part Alvin was too modest to mention: "He's one of the Indian Rodeo Cowboy Association's top award-winners. He has four championship saddles and over fifty silver and gold championship buckles."

Jeweler Hank Whitethorne is also a bareback bronc rider. "I've been a professional rodeo rider for about seventeen years," he said. "I ride in rodeos all over, even Canada." In March of 1993, Hank's home burned and he and his family lost everything, even his tools and raw materials. "We'll start over," Hank said, but he shook his head sadly as he added, "I lost all my trophies and buckles." Gibson Nez rode saddle broncs during his twenty years of rodeoing and, in 1980, was inducted into the All Indian Cowboy Hall of Fame in Window Rock. Rodeoing is a tough act to get out of your system. Most of these "cowboys" started out as little boys herding sheep. Fidel Bahe laughed as he recalled his sheepherding days.

"We didn't have toys. I played with rocks, but that's when your imagination kicks in. I built corrals for stink bugs. I'd find eight or ten of them and stick them in there. They were my cattle. That's how I learned to be creative and to use my hands."—FIDEL BAHE

"I lived right across the hill from David Johns. We both had to take our sheep out, and we'd get our herds all mixed up. Our folks would get mad; they'd have to spend half a day trying to divide up the sheep. We didn't have toys. I played with rocks, but that's when your imagination kicks in. I built corrals for stink bugs. I'd find eight or ten of them and stick them in there. They were my cattle. That's how I learned to be creative and to use my hands."

"We learned from watching," Robert Henry Jr. said. "My grandfather and father were both silversmiths and my grandmother was a weaver. As a young boy, I helped her set up the loom. She would tell me how everything was done and I watched her weave her rugs from start to finish."

It was all simply a part of the Navajo Way, and Nelson Tsosie expressed it well when speaking of his father being a silversmith, his mother and grandmother being weavers: "It wasn't called art; it was called living."

More than any other art form, rug weaving is part of the pastoral Navajo life, and the loom is what many artists recall when they think of their childhood. Baje Whitethorne remembers his "grandmother, two aunts, and my mother all sitting in a row weaving on one huge rug."

Redwing Nez pointed toward his grandmother's house on the hill above his studio. "They would have two looms going right up there," he said. "The ladies would weave together and talk. While Grandma Lucy weaved, kids were born, goats got lost, life went on—the only things that were important were what went on in this valley. The daily solving of problems was woven right into her rugs."

"While Grandma Lucy weaved, kids were born, goats got lost, life went on—the only things that were important were what went on in this valley. The daily solving of problems was woven right into her rugs."—REDWING NEZ

THE NAVAJO LIFESTYLE APPEARS in all mediums, as artists express their emotions about the land and the People. "My pastels reflect my life experiences as taught to me by my grandparents," painter Jack To'Baahe Gene says. "They were my primary influences and helped me to understand and respect my culture."

"My mother's a weaver," Clifford Beck said. "She's been weaving all her life. Someday I want to paint her in her surroundings, with the land. She taught us everything we needed to know about tribal customs and values and religious beliefs. Even to this day, I hold these things with respect. I guess that's why my works are of older people, and my subjects are traditional."

"I have always had a love for art," Shonto Begay said. "I drew from nature and developed a strong bond with the sights around me. A piece of driftwood, an old gray boulder, a dead bird, a bare wood hogan—these were not mere sights. They became part of my visions and emotions."

Visions and emotions are shared by many artists, through sculpture as well as painting. "I represent events in my life by symbolism," Alvin Marshall said. "I herded sheep and slept out under the stars as a child. I want my sculptures to represent what was and what is—and I want people to pause and reflect on them."

Sculpture is very much a fledgling art among the Navajo, and Larry Yazzie explained the probable reason. "The only stonework the old Navajos did was to make the small fetishes for medicine bundles," he said. "Sculpture is very new to them and a lot of traditional people think it's wrong. To the traditional Navajo,

OPPOSITE: *Crystal style weaving by Irene Clark, 61" by 44". Usually woven in earth tones and muted colors, Crystal rugs are characterized by three bands of wavy lines or a solid color between complex bands featuring squash blossoms, arrows, stars, crosses, diamonds, and other motifs.*

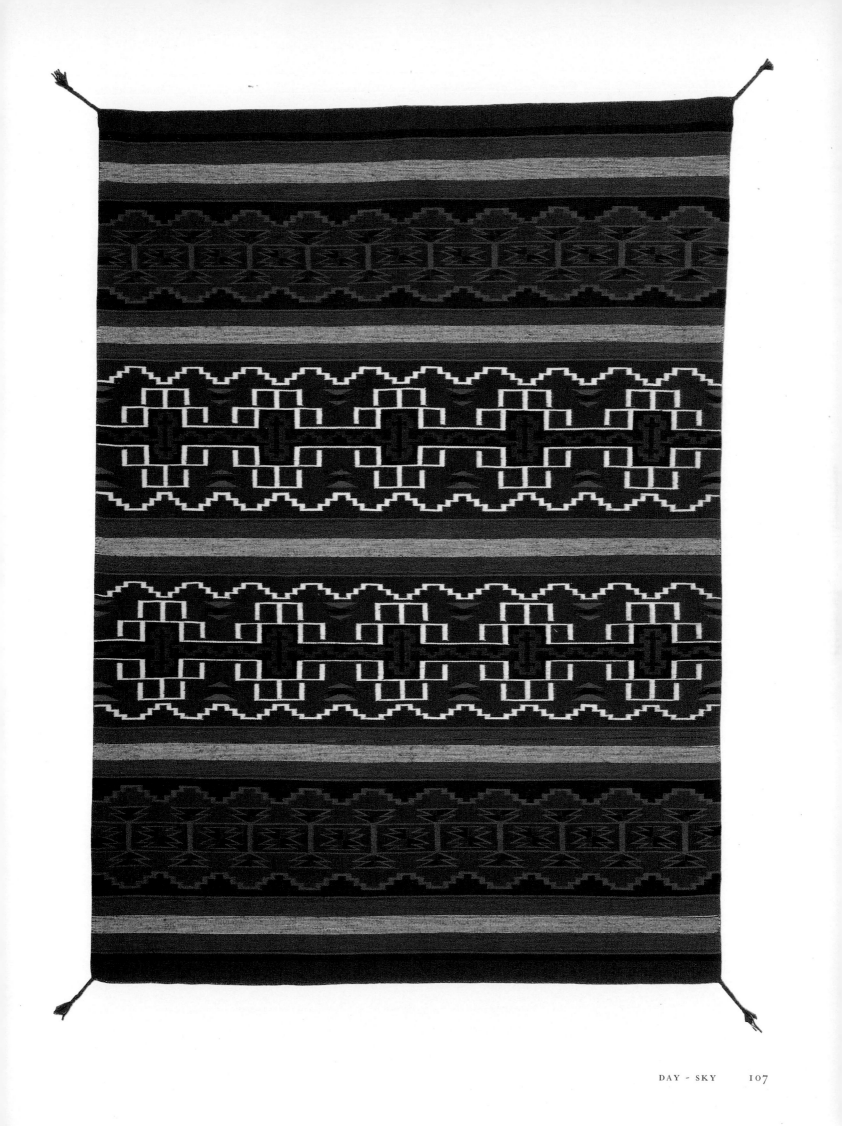

stone is very sacred. Only the medicine men gathered it, and they always left some and said a prayer where the stone was found. It is part of the earth, and everything on earth is sacred. We must stay in harmony. If you don't keep things in balance, it starts coming back on you. The old people told me that because I use the stones, I must have a Beauty Way—to the mountains, the water, and Mother Earth. It needs to be done about every two years.

"The old people told me that because I use the stones, I must have a Beauty Way—to the mountains, the water, and Mother Earth."—LARRY YAZZIE

OPPOSITE: Celebration of Life *is a unique one-piece wood carving (14" tall) by David V. Draper. The piece represents the life of a Navajo couple from the time of their first vows. Beginning at the bottom, the trail winds upward as a migration from the flat country, the desert. As the Diné have done for centuries, the couple moves their herds to the higher and cooler elevation during the summer months. When fall arrives, the trek back to the lower and warmer climate begins. The images of the Corn People on the back of the piece symbolize both fertility and the planting of vegetation. The rain and cloud designs above the Corn People represent moisture and prosperity. The left hand is symbolic of Left-Handed, a man of the* Bitahni *clan, who holds four kernels of corn representing the Four Sacred Directions and their colors.*

"My clan sister is a stargazer. She told me to take a couple of small pieces of alabaster and always carry them with me. They represent the stone. I say a prayer while holding the stones to show my respect. We are told that we must always be gentle with the stone; I have to be careful what I'm thinking about when carving, and watch what I say. I really learned these things from the stone before she even told me."

Faced with this nascent art, Navajo sculptors are still trying their wings. Although some use marble, steatite, and other stones, as well as metal, bronze, and ceramics, most carve from alabaster, which comes in a variety of colors and is enhanced by interesting striations. Most also depict traditional subjects, which are carved realistically.

Fred Begay, however, is one who believes that "less is more." "I try to simplify," he said. "When I work with form, I try to find the simplest line to follow. Sketching is drawing just the outline of subjects. That's where my sculpture comes from."

"I look into the stone," Harold Davidson said, "and think how I can make it live. I try to put myself into the place of the people who will look at the piece. Does it mean something? What's going to happen next? Am I putting all of myself into it? That's what makes a piece."

"Stone has its own image," Roy Walters declared. "It has a life quality and spirit of its own. It's part of the earth as we are, but it knows no sin. It is positive, and I base my work on a positive image."

Tim Washburn believes that "you have to be a student all your life. Once you think you know it all, you've had it. I had very good teachers. I learned from Alvin Marshall and Oreland Joe."

In searching for the beginnings of sculpture among the Navajo, all roads eventually lead back to Oreland Joe—less than fifteen short years ago. "There's been sculpture in Santa Fe for years," Oreland said, "and in Taos and along the Rio Grande, but I guess I started it in our corner of the world. When I went to IAIA in 1980, there were no other Navajo sculptors there. I only stayed six days. I don't mean to put down the school; it just wasn't the way I pictured it. I went home and tore pictures from *Southwest Art* and studied anything that had to do with sculpture. I experimented and learned on my own. A few friends—Alvin Marshall, Tim Washburn, Greg Johnson—came along who wanted to learn

and I taught them the basics. Then in 1984, I was asked to teach a sculpture workshop at Shiprock High School. I did that for three years and, a few years later, sculpture began showing up in trading posts and stores. The sad thing is that it's being treated as a craft. Only a few of the many doing sculpture today will stay. They will study hard and improve; to the others, it's just a money-making venture."

The sculptural art of kachina doll carving is rooted in Hopi and other Pueblo religions. Because the replication of their sacred kachinas by others is considered blasphemy by most Puebloans, we have chosen to omit such carvings by Navajos. A few Navajo artists, however, have mastered the art of wood carving and create beautiful works that are indicative of their own culture. David Draper is one of these carvers who has received awards in numerous Indian art exhibitions. His one-piece wood sculpture, *Celebration of Life,* ideally illustrates Day-Sky.

IT IS SUMMER, a time of fruitfulness and growth, a time to celebrate life. Artists continue to mature as they walk the trail of Beauty and, as each day moves inexorably on toward evening, their art continues to evolve.

Coming Home. *Twenty-seven-year-old Ronald Benally carved this 46" long alabaster sculpture, which won First Prize and Best of Category at the 1993 Gallup Intertribal Indian Ceremonial. "This sculpture came mainly from my mom," Ronald said. "The Navajo relied on sheep. The more sheep you had, the wealthier you were. Sheep provided everything for the old traditional people."*

EVENING-TWILIGHT

I am walking along the trail

I am walking along the trail

Before me, it is blessed

I am walking along the trail

Behind me, it is blessed

I am walking along the trail

Above me, it is blessed

I am walking along the trail

Below me, it is blessed

I am walking along the trail

All around me, it is blessed

I am walking along the trail

On the trail it is beautiful

I am walking along the trail

—from The Blessingway

ABOVE: Generations, *a 40" by 56" oil on canvas by Clifford Beck, won First Prize at the 1993 Santa Fe Indian Market.*

PREVIOUS PAGE: Reed Valley, *a 30" by 22" painting by Baje Whitethorne Sr., is in colored pencil, prisma color, and acrylics. "My clan is the Reed Clan,"* Baje *says. "I was born out there; it's where I grew up. When I sit down to sketch, I see it all again in my mind's eye. I see the colors; I start to paint and it all just happens."*

EVENING-TWILIGHT

White blooms cascade from tall yucca stalks glistening in the late afternoon sunlight that streams across a vast landscape, spotlighting a sandstone spire rising into an azure sky. Sunlight and shadows play hide-and-seek in the quiet canyon below. Suddenly, the countryside is infused with the soft, yellow-evening-glow of Navajo legend.

The still, silent land whispers of timelessness as it weaves a magic born of the breeze riffling the sand dunes, of red cliffs and spires turning to flame in the evening light, of the hawk circling high above.

Sheep are herded into home corrals and small birds flit and flutter from tree to tree in search of a resting place for the night. The aroma of juniper smoke drifts in as the dinner hour approaches and, as twilight deepens, the calm hush is broken only by the occasional bleat of a lamb.

It is Evening-Twilight, a family time. Like morning, this is a time that is good, a time when offerings are made. Evening is symbolic of autumn, and the walk along life's Trail of Beauty has reached another plateau.

In the autumn of life priorities often change; family becomes of more concern than career, spirituality more significant than self, nature more important than the trappings of wealth.

Although it seems something of a paradox, at this time of maturity an artist's work may become fresh and new. It is a time when many artists return to their homeland, choosing reservation homes over the convenience and comfort of urban areas. Some, such as sculptor Larry Yazzie, see it as an opportunity to raise their children away from the cities with their inherent problems and to instill in them the tenets of the Navajo Way.

DOWRY, *13" by 19" watercolor By Elizabeth Whitethorne-Benally. "I was greatly influenced by the women in my family and clan, women who are very independent and strong," Elizabeth said. "The women in all of my paintings are very personal. I painted this piece when my husband and I were married in 1991. This was a time of intense growth in my life."*

"We're moving back to the reservation," Larry said softly. "We have four boys and I'm seeing how important it is for them to learn the culture, the language, the values. You can't really learn it off the reservation. You need to be around the grandparents to pick it all up. I have an uncle who is a medicine man for the Night Dance, my wife's grandfather is a Beauty Way medicine man, and another uncle is in the Native American Church. We have a family legacy of medicine people, and we're realizing just how important these things are to us. The old people are the only ones who know the medicine 'ways,' and they are passing on. Learning the ceremonies are too difficult for the younger ones. It's a lifelong commitment; you have to really believe in it.

"It's a big decision for us, this moving back, but we've decided our culture has to come first. Our language, our traditions, and our culture are being lost so quickly. We want to do something—for us and our children."

Other artists visit the reservation often. Baje Whitethorne, who lives in Flagstaff, says, "when I come up against a 'painter's block,' I just go home to the reservation. I'm reborn and refreshed by the stories I once heard, the rocks I played on; it all comes back."

"They have each given me a little bit of what they know."—ELIZABETH WHITETHORNE-BENALLY

Back among the sandstone pinnacles and monoliths, sculptors find inspiration for modern works of art. The incredible evening light and the subtle shades of color inspire others to turn to paint and canvas. A ceremony stirs the emotions and a sandpainter begins trickling tiny grains of sand between nimble fingers. As mountain peaks glow in the late evening light, a jeweler sits down at his workbench; wildlife fires the imagination and a potter reaches for clay; a weaver carries the image of the storm with her as she weaves thundercloud symbols into an intricate design.

It is evening, the time when families join together again after being apart all day. Among the Navajo, the strong family bond never weakens, and may well be another reason for such a proliferation of Navajo artists.

It is not unusual for families to have seven, ten, perhaps fourteen children, all of whom become artists. One family may include silversmiths, weavers, painters, and potters. The nine children of Alice (a weaver) and Leonard Whitethorne are all artists—painters, potters, and one silversmith. "I remember lying on the dirt floor of the hogan," Elizabeth Whitethorne-Benally recalls, "coloring by kerosene light. My older brothers would take my picture away and try to show me how to shade it correctly. They have each given me a little bit of what they know."

One of those brothers is Baje Whitethorne Sr., an outstanding contemporary artist. Baje's art has several distinct trademarks: his whimsical, animated people, his unique landscapes with colorful ebullient skies, and his blue chair. Told by an art professor to "put something personal into your work," Baje proceeded to do so. He remembered an old blue folding chair from his childhood. "When I'd come in hot from school or herding sheep, it always felt so cool against my legs.

Sometimes I'd lay my face against it. But it seems like I always had to look for it. Nobody really hid it, it just kept getting moved around." Now the blue chair appears in most of Baje's paintings. Sometimes, it's in plain view, sometimes behind a post or the hogan with just some part of it showing: it's usually there somewhere; one just has to find it.

Hank is another Whitethorne who is noted for his artistry. He and his wife, Olivia, set colorful stones into massive silver jewelry that is reminiscent of Aztec art. However, Hank's symbolism comes from Navajo ceremonies and legends. "Some of my designs can't be explained in English," Hank said, "only Navajo. There are no English words to describe them." Perhaps that is because there is no need; one can simply enjoy their beauty.

Twenty-five-year-old Charles Morris learned his basic silversmithing techniques from his father, but then changed his style. "My father said that I should try my oil painting skills on silver, the way the Hopi do," Charles said. "I learned as I went along. My father helped all he could, but he didn't really know much about it either. I had no one to tell me if what I was doing was right or wrong. Now my little sister is showing an interest. She'll have an advantage that I didn't have because I can help her. But I can take her just so far; her art has to come from the inside."

Although Tsosie Taylor's father was a silversmith, Tsosie is one who learned his skills from siblings. "I wasn't around my father too much," he said. "I learned from my brother Herbert and my sister and brother-in-law, Anita and Gary Gene. It came in handy; it was my jewelry that helped support me through college."

"Now my little sister is showing an interest. She'll have an advantage that I didn't have because I can help her. But I can take her just so far; her art has to come from the inside."—CHARLES MORRIS

"I've been sketching and drawing since I was seven or eight," Virgil Nez said. "I had older twin brothers who went to IAIA. I used to copy them, and one of them, Ervin, helped me some." Although Virgil was an architecture major, his plans changed and he earned his degree in illustration and painting.

At nine, Vernon Begaye started helping his parents, both silversmiths. "I did the polishing," he said. "It was a family effort. All seven kids were involved in helping some way."

Both of Vernon Haskie's parents were also silversmiths and, when he was five, Vernon asked his father an interesting question. "Why are you pounding on that [silver] so hard?" Vernon laughed as he added, "He told me he was making money. I couldn't figure out how he made money by pounding on metal. But for Christmas, my brother and I got new Tonka trucks; I went out and pounded mine flat with a hammer. When my mother got on me about it, I told her I was trying to make money. That's when my father gave me some silver to pound." Now Vernon creates beautiful overlay and shadowbox jewelry, using techniques he learned on his own. "My dad kept stressing stamp work, but I wasn't interested. One day my folks went to town and I soldered my first piece while they were gone. I'd watched my dad do it. It was just a small ring, but I inlaid it with chip inlay [a process his father had learned from Tommy Singer], and had it done before they got back. As time passed, I experimented a lot and consulted with other artists and people in the business. When you're self-taught, you learn a lot of tricks. Some things I learned were already known by other artists, some I think are special to me. I'm inspired by other artists like Harvey Begay and James Little, and Charles Loloma's quotes make a lot of sense. I read where he said, 'If you want to create art, use your best materials.' I immediately switched to the highest grade of metal and the best stones."

"When you're self-taught, you learn a lot of tricks. Some things I learned were already known by other artists, some I think are special to me."—VERNON HASKIE

Mary Black, the catalyst in her basketmaking family, taught ten of her twelve children and two daughters-in-law to weave. With the encouragement of Utah traders Barry and Steve Simpson, Mary and her family are creating basketry with unique designs. Through the years, most Navajo basketweavers have used geometrics similar to those on wedding baskets. Within the last ten years or so, a few other designs, such as butterflies and eagles, have begun to appear. However, the Simpsons challenged the basketweavers in the Monument Valley area to begin using Navajo symbolism based upon traditional beliefs.

"As we read more about Navajo mythology," Barry explained, "we got more excited. We began to talk to some of the younger weavers about certain stories. They might not be familiar with a particular one, but they would go home and ask the elders about it. As the old stories came out, they became excited about including these subjects, such as Changing Woman and Monster Slayer, in their baskets. Some of these designs haven't been used because of certain taboos, but now weavers are beginning to push the boundaries to the limit."

"As they question the older people about the legends," Steve added, "they are learning more about their own culture and are becoming more traditional. They're sort of coming into it by the back door."

Barry smiled and nodded. "Although it goes against the traditional Navajo Way, they're becoming very competitive. In fact, the weaving on Mary's baskets was getting larger and her designs weren't as good as before. I thought the years were beginning to catch up with her, but when Sally and Lorraine began winning awards and prize money, Mary suddenly popped back. Now she's coming up with some great baskets. And she knows all the old legends. She knows some of the symbolism that the younger ones don't know. Mary's baskets always have a story and every line has meaning."

"As they got excited about using their own designs in their baskets instead of copying from others," Steve said, "they also became more concerned about quality. Instead of using the normal five rods of sumac, they switched to three, which

makes a finer weave and much nicer designs. Of course, it also takes more time and the baskets demand a higher price."

"Navajo baskets are traditionally made of sumac," Barry explained. "They leave the bark on the branches that are used for the weaving rods. This adds strength and stability to the basket. The branches used for weaving have the bark removed and are split into strips of the desired width. For the most part, colors are obtained with aniline dyes."

"There was an explosion of new styles and designs in Navajo weaving; today that explosion is taking place in basketry."—BARRY SIMPSON

OPPOSITE: *These baskets, ranging in size from 13 3/4" to 16 1/2" diameter were woven by Mary Black and four of her daughters. Mary was the recipient of the 1993 Utah Governor's Folk Art Award as an artist who has revitalized a traditional art form. Clockwise from top: Mary's basket design recreates the Fire Dance of the Navajo. Fires burn between each of the six fire dancers and the green crosses represent brush arbors that are erected for many ceremonies. Agnes Gray portrayed Changing Woman and the two arrows of the Hero Twins. Sally Black wove the eagle basket. Lorraine Black's pictorial basket has a turtle in the center, surrounded by a man, a pickup, a hogan, three dogs, and a saddled horse. Cora Black wove the sandpainting basket with the sun, two yei'iis, corn stalks, four sets of feathers, and rainbow designs symbolic of the Four Directions.*

"The evolution of baskets is about fifty years behind rugs," Barry added, "but the evolutionary path is the same. There was an explosion of new styles and designs in Navajo weaving; today that explosion is taking place in basketry."

"Mary's family is unbelievable," Steve chimed in. "Just as we think we've seen everything, they spring something new on us."

Another creative family is that of Carl Taylor, the elderly Navajo *hataałi* who allowed photography of the contents of his medicine bundle. Twice married (both times to weavers), Carl was a traditional silversmith in the early years. His progeny includes several weavers, and four sons and one daughter who followed in his footsteps. The three sons featured here have developed contemporary styles.

Tsosie is a cross-country runner and the first of the family to graduate from college. "I've only been making jewelry about five years," Tsosie said. "I don't really know too much yet; I'm still learning." He is overly modest; he and his wife, Mary, do exquisite work, and their unusual "modified" squash blossom-style necklace won first prize at the 1992 Santa Fe Indian Market. The designs of this overlay necklace are adapted from those in the Crystal-style rugs created by Tsosie's mother, Lillian. "My mom is in her eighties," Tsosie said. "She doesn't weave much anymore; she just takes care of her sheep and goats now. The necklace was a tribute to her."

Herbert creates outstanding contemporary jewelry and is noted for his use of high-grade American turquoise stones. "When I can't come up with a design, I just think back. I remember something from my past and I can start working again. All Navajo art comes from our way of life—our ceremonies. Everything fits together. My dad always told me that when I sell a piece of jewelry, a part of me leaves with the one I sold it to. I need to have a ceremony every so often. That's the only way to create new and better designs. I get a mental block when my designs leave with the people."

Like Herbert, Robert works in both gold and silver, often combining the two. Images of hogans, horses, wagons, and livestock trail around his bracelets and rings and across concho belts. "I remember my dad making jewelry in the old days," Robert explained. "We lived in a hogan with no water or electricity, and us kids herded the sheep. I thought of those things, and started making my 'storyteller' designs. I like to try different things."

At times Robert adorns his jewelry with *yei'iis,* the prehistoric flute player, or rug designs. Each concho of a belt he made in 1993 represents a different weaving pattern. "It takes a lot of time to come up with rug designs and they're a lot of work," Robert said. "My wife, Christine, is a weaver; she designed the rugs on the concho belt."

Family relationships influence artists in many ways. Rosie Yellowhair says she began doing sandpaintings because she is from a long line of medicine people. "My grandfather was a medicine man, then my uncle, now my dad. I saw things done in the ceremonies that intrigued me."

"When I can't come up with a design, I just think back. I remember something from my past and I can start working again."—HERBERT TAYLOR

Lillie T. Taylor, wife of Carl and mother of Herbert and Robert, wove this unusual 60" by 37" rug she calls Sunset Yei'ii.

ABOVE: *Tsosie and Mary Taylor won First Prize at the 1992 Santa Fe Indian Market with this contemporary squash blossom—style necklace set. It was made in honor of Tsosie's mother, and designs were adapted from those in her Crystal rugs. The naja represents the rainbow; the clasp is a butterfly.*

RIGHT: *Herbert Taylor is noted for his use of only the best stones in his exquisite jewelry. The 14-karat bola tie is set with Indian Mountain turquoise and ironwood; the 18-karat gold necklace (left) is set with Nevada blue turquoise and ironwood; and the 18-karat gold necklace (right) has coral and Indian Mountain turquoise in the pendant, Sleeping Beauty turquoise in its links.*

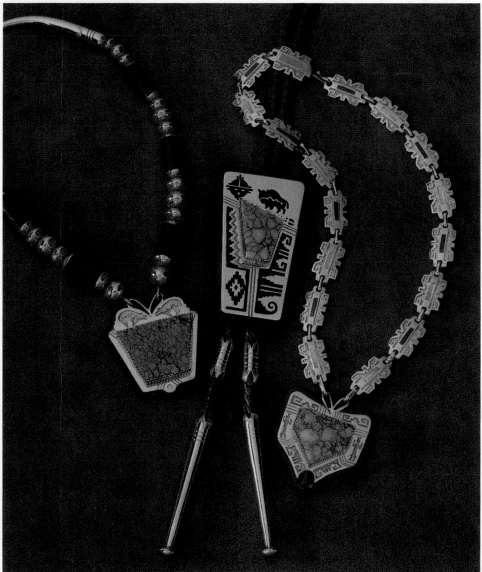

THIS PAGE AND OPPOSITE: *The designs on the gold "story" bracelet by Robert Taylor (opposite) are based on traditional Navajo lifestyle; the flute player with the bola tie is an ancient Anasazi figure. Designed by Robert's wife, Christine Nelson, each concho of the gold-over-silver belt has a different rug style. Christine and her sister, Victoria Keoni, created the rugs pictured on this page. Both rugs have similar patterns, but Christine's 30 1/2" by 55 1/2" rug (below) is a Ganado and Victoria's is a Burntwater, 35" by 61". Both of these styles were included in the design of Robert's belt.*

ABOVE: Twin Sisters, *a 24" by 30"*
oil on canvas by James King (Bée-Ditt'o).

RIGHT: *Jewelry by brothers Lee*
(necklace and earrings) and Raymond
(bracelets) Yazzie.

This 63" by 96" Teec Nos Pos weaving is by Cara Whitney.

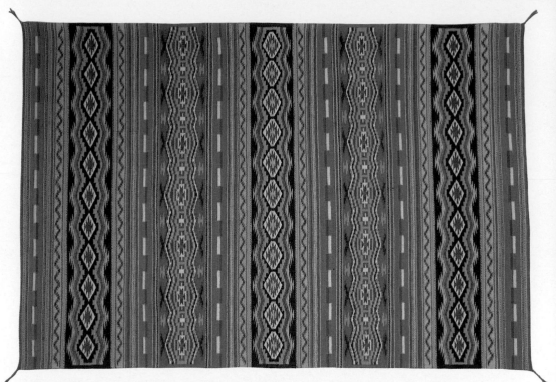

RIGHT AND OPPOSITE: *Wide Ruins style weavings by mother and daughter Betty B. Roan and Jennie Thomas. Betty wove the 41" by 59 1/2" rug pictured at right. Jennie created the 41" by 25" tapestry-quality rug shown opposite, which combines an intricate Wide Ruins design with Burntwater colors.*

IN THE NAVAJO WALK, Evening is a time when many artists begin to search for something new and different, and Mary Morez says her "ideas come from a thirst for knowledge": "My brain is like an endless sky and I have to use it. Nobody has copied my work. Of course, I use rice paper, which is a challenge. No one knows exactly how I do it and I want to keep it that way. There's something very personal about art, and I don't care to expose everything. If you tell all you know, you become an empty vessel."

"My brain is like an endless sky and I have to use it."—MARY MOREZ

European artists of the seventeenth and eighteenth centuries, particularly Pia Castellani, are the inspiration for Carl and Irene Clark's micro-fine inlay jewelry. "The stones are meticulously hand-ground to minute sizes to fit together into a mosaic pattern," Carl explained. "I use the fine inlay as the picture and the silver or gold metalwork as the frame. I purposely mix my colors or the shades of different stones to emphasize the fineness of the inlay."

Peter Ray James attended IAIA, where he became enamoured with the work of T. C. Canon. "I dreamed that we met. It was a very spiritual journey, and I still do a lot of circles in homage to his work."

Shonto Begay says, "My large paintings are a series of brushstrokes, small strokes that repeat like the words of a Blessingway prayer. The process becomes a visual chant."

Jennifer Musial "uses the colors of the mountain and horizons" in her weaving. "My mom and I prefer our own colors to that we find in the stores. We use natural and commercial wool about fifty-fifty, but buy the commercial wool undyed and dye it ourselves. My grandmother has a few sheep and Mom's sisters and aunts also save some of the best wool for us. We sometimes spend a week just carding wool, but my grandmother does most of the spinning. We love dyeing, just to see what comes out."

Red Dream: Return from the Long Walk, a 50" by 50" painting by W. B. Franklin. "I took a trip to Ft. Sumner (Bosque Redondo) just before I did this painting," he said. "As I walked around there, I thought of the tribu- lations and hardships my ancestors suffered during their four years of imprisonment. But I also thought about their return home and how happy they and the spirits were because they were finally back between the Four Sacred Mountains. This is what the painting is about. The red in the painting represents the earth."

Fertile Ground, *28 1/4" by 40 1/2" pastel on paper on canvas by Emmi Whitehorse. "My paintings are all about my experiences," Emmi says. "I'm very affected by my surroundings. Our summer home was not in a lush area where just anything would grow. Nothing came easy. We had drought in summer, too much snow and mud in winter. This painting represents a longing for what we didn't have."*

The beads of Ray Scott's exceptional silver jewelry have a beautiful, unusual texture. When questioned about it, he grinned almost sheepishly. "My brother is a machinist, so I use some of his tools. The beads are shaved in a ball-bearing machine."

Ingenious and talented, Navajo artists are quick to use anything that works for them. Fidel Bahe makes his jewelry tools "from old files, horseshoe nails, piston rods, anything that will reharden and take a temper." Fidel's jewelry, although basically traditional, has very contemporary aspects, and his workmanship is excellent. "I love what I do too much to take shortcuts," he said. "I have to give it my personal best."

Other artists strive for the best while branching out into other areas of art. Baje Whitethorne has illustrated two delightful children's books based on Navajo legends, *Monster Slayer* and *Monster Birds,* and he wrote and illustrated *Sunpainters.* Shonto Begay illustrated both *The Mud Pony* and *Mai'ii and Cousin Horned Toad,* and was also the author of the latter. For this effort, he received the 1993 Arizona Author Award, which is presented for "excellence in writing and illustration for children and young adults." Clifford Brycelea has illustrated covers for Louis L'Amour's books, and Ernest Franklin's illustrations are very much in demand; his humorous look at *Navajo Taboos* is outstanding.

Mountain Dance Spirit, a *29" tall*
contemporary sculpture by Robert Dale
Tsosie, is made of Belgian marble and inlaid
with Nevada spiderweb turquoise.

Joe Ben Jr.'s experience with the commercial art world is somewhat different. Instead of the contemporary sandpaintings or ceremonial scenes he normally does, he was commissioned to do a sandpainting of a landscape scene for a Toyota promotion in 1993. That year also led Joe into an entirely new field, one that he enjoyed immensely. During the NBA finals, he announced the Phoenix Suns' games live, in Navajo, for Window Rock's radio station KTNN.

Creative people are often willing to try other avenues of expression, and Redwing Nez plunged into acting at the "deep end of the pool." He was one of the lead warriors in Kevin Costner's *Dances With Wolves.* "I've got it in my blood," Redwing said. "That was excitment! Riding a horse at thirty-five or forty miles an hour in the middle of a herd of buffalo, checking to make sure Kevin was all right riding next to me, the dust and the noise. What a rush! When I was a kid out herding sheep, I used to pretend the tumbleweeds were buffalo, and I chased them all over the place. I finally got to chase the real thing! But it was work. I started out on the buffalo hunt in the morning trying to look good," Redwing added with a grin. "By the end of the day I was just trying to hang on. But it taught me some respect for those old guys who rode like that all the time in the past. When I get ready to paint, I have to go back into it again in my mind—the dust, the noise, the buffalo, the thrill. That's what excites you in painting—the feeling. It must be in the soul before it can come out in art."

"That's what excites you in painting—the feeling. It must be in the soul before it can come out in art."——REDWING NEZ

Easel artists today produce paintings in every medium and in a variety of different styles; however, this type of art is relatively new to the Navajo. An interesting quote from Frances E. Watkins in a small publication entitled *Southwest Museum Leaflets* #16 demonstrates just how far easel art has come in a relatively short time. The booklet is undated but, judging from its content, was probably published in the late 1930s. "Navajo art, in the sense of painting and sculpture, is expressed only in the form of ceremonial dry painting, traced with colored earth according to ancient tradition.

"Of late years, however, a number of young artists have begun the use of a new medium, and their watercolors of Navajo life and Navajo scenes possess an unusual individuality in color and rhythm. . . . The quality of some of the young men, particularly Gerald Nailor and Tohoma, is marked by flowing lines, unusual color combinations, and delicacy of detail, forming compositions of richness and strength. Primitive as these pictures may be, there is nothing crude nor inartistic about them. They are merely an indication of what these particularly endowed people may accomplish in the future."

What "these particularly endowed people" have accomplished to date is apparent in realistic portrayals of cultural scenes, landscapes, sacred images, and ceremonies. As most Navajo art comes from very emotional memories, even abstract designs have a serenity and beauty not often found in the modern art of other cultures. Art that does include a hint of the abstract is usually composed of

ABOVE: *A 32" by 42" acrylic on canvas by David Johns. Entitled* The Couple, *it represents a man and woman, wrapped in a blanket, walking in the moonlight.*

OPPOSITE: *Bronze sculptures by Larry L. Yazzie. The original of* Into the Sky *(left), 30" tall, was carved from Utah alabaster;* Beauty All Around Me, *28 1/2" tall, was cast from an original of Virginia steatite. Larry says that his sculptures often portray women because "the woman symbolizes life and the foundation of the family. The wedding basket represents the union of male and female."*

graceful, flowing lines and pleasing colors that create a sense of harmony. Because that harmony is necessary to a good life, most Navajo artists have no desire to include discord and strife in their work.

When David Johns, who does wonderful abstract paintings, was commissioned to do a mural in a Phoenix office building, that very subject was broached by a visitor. "While I was painting the mural," David said, "an American Indian from another part of the country came in and asked to speak to me. He told me that I was wrong to portray spiritual images and that I should only paint controversial subjects or make a statement about injustice to Indian people. This really upset me. I told him that I could not do that. I wanted to honor my people with this mural."

Contemporary Navajo painting is an open door that invites the viewer to enter. One can see the beauty of David Johns' abstract designs, but understanding their underlying message brings a deeper appreciation. "My landscapes are all color and light," David explained, "the colors of the sand, the bushes, the red rock country, the sunset sky. I can see lines in landscapes that interchange, some horizontal, some vertical, some angled. Most people don't realize the lines are there." His work often includes "thundercloud symbols that move across the earth, producing rain and bringing harmony between Mother Earth and Father

Sky" and his sweeping colors may "capture the intense colors of a sunset during a rainstorm."

Yet, as Wallace Begay says "there is part of art that we don't define. We paint it and have something new to say to the viewer. I try to put something into my art that you can't quite put your finger on. Put a little mystery in. That gives it life and adds interest, draws the viewer in."

"There is part of art that we don't define. We paint it and have something new to say to the viewer."—WALLACE BEGAY

Maiden in Waiting, *a 22" tall strawberry alabaster sculpture by Leslie Pablo.*

Larry Yazzie's graceful sculptures also leave something to the imagination, but he did explain why he usually portrays women. "To me, the woman symbolizes life and the foundation of the family. In the Navajo Way, my grandmother taught me that wealth isn't in what you own; it is in children. Throughout life you struggle to raise a family, but at the end you have children to be there and care for you. Navajo women have a lot of inner strength."

The "inner strength, beauty, and dignity" of women is what Elizabeth Abeyta portrays in her clay sculptures. "But I'm breaking away from the older styles to keep from getting burned out," she said. "Things are coming together for me, and I'm getting more confident. I want to get away from that stereotype of two Indian girls gazing into the sky."

"I was greatly influenced by the women in my family, women who are very independent and strong," Elizabeth Whitethorne-Benally said. "As a very young woman, I got a chance to spend a lot of time with my great-grandmother. She showed me who I am and my position in the family; she taught me to be independent and self-reliant. I learned from her and my mother and grandmother that everything goes from the female side of the family."

This is literally true. Navajo society is matrilineal, and children are born "to" the mother's clan and "for" the father's. One who sees only the surface of the

THIS PAGE: *The pottery of both Ida Sahmie and Christine Nofchissey McHorse is influenced by their husbands' families. Ida Sahmie learned the art of pottery-making from her mother-in-law, Priscilla Namingha (whose great-grandmother was the famous Tewa-Hopi potter Nampeyo), but was encouraged to use designs from her own Navajo culture. Although the clay that she uses and the shapes of her vessels often come from her husband's Hopi tradition, Ida's designs remain her own. Adorned with yei'ii figures and wedding baskets, this unusual piece (bottom right) is 5 3/4" tall and 7 1/2" in diameter. Christine Nofchissey McHorse learned pottery-making from her husband's grandmother, Lena Archuleta of Taos Pueblo. But Christine has gone far beyond those early teachings to blend micaceous clay from that area with her own highly contemporary styles. Her versatility is shown in the group of pottery pictured at top right. Clockwise from upper left: jar with appliquéd and incised lightning designs and incised cloud and rain symbols; corrugated jar; melon-shaped jar with incised designs; "story" jar with appliquéd figures and incised designs around the shoulder. All but the corrugated jar are coated with a fine layer of pitch.*

OPPOSITE: *The simple elegance of pottery by Alice W. Cling. These pieces range in height from 4 1/2" to 8".*

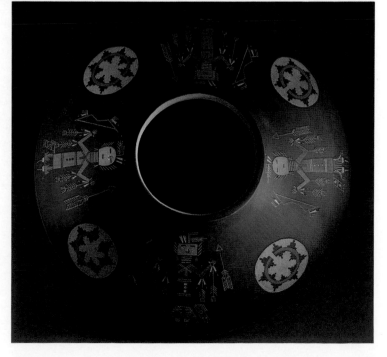

Samuel Manymules uses traditional
techniques to create a simple but highly
sophisticated style of pottery that blends
graceful shapes with unusual colors and
beautiful fire clouds resulting from the firing
process. The pieces range in height from
5" to 18 1/2".

All vegetal dyes were used in this striking 72" by 54" Burntwater style weaving by Maggie Price. Burntwater weavers typically weave in a wide variety of vegetal-dyed colors and combine earth tones and pastels in creating intricate geometric patterns.

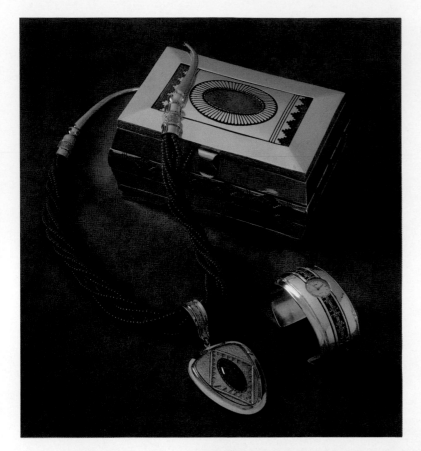

LEFT: *Al Joe made this silver box set with blue gem turquoise, the gold and coral necklace, and the silver watch bracelet.*

BELOW: *Jewelry by Victor Beck. The artist refers to the bola tie as his "Santa Fe style." The necklace may be worn with either the coral strands or the turquoise beads in front, or turned to show a portion of both. With added clasps, either section may also be worn separately as a choker. The cluster of four different beads on the left side of the necklace represents the Four Directions: white shell for the East; turquoise for the South; abalone for the West; and jet for the North.*

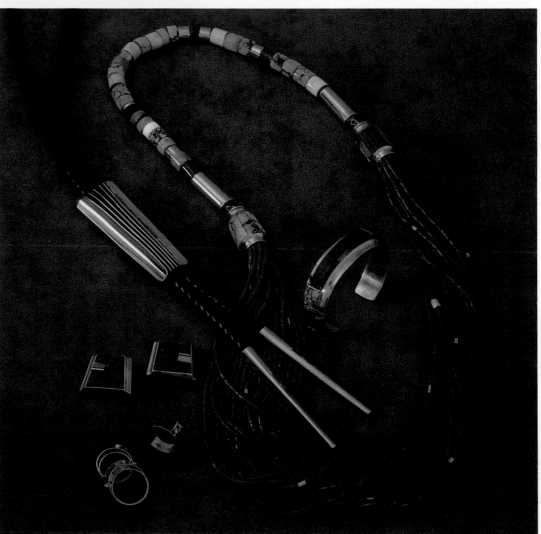

Navajo culture might question the women's status, but the Navajo woman knows the importance of her place in society and has no need to flaunt it.

"Indian women are liberated the day they are born," Mary Morez declared. "Who's going to saddle the horse, repair the roof, and haul the water when there's no man around? That's liberation, baby. In our society, the woman is the dominant figure who becomes the wise one in her old age. But she never demands her status. She achieves, earns, accomplishes it through maturity. That maturing process is psychological. It has to do with one's feelings for the land and being part of the whole cycle of nature."

"In our society, the woman is the dominant figure who becomes the wise one in her old age. She achieves, earns, accomplishes [her status] through maturity."—MARY MOREZ

The influence of Navajo women on the art world is demonstrated in the contemporary pottery of Christine McHorse, who learned to make pottery from her husband's grandmother, Lena Archuleta of Taos Pueblo. "She first taught me how to make pottery," Christine said, "but I worked my techniques out for

Gold and silver jewelry by Howard Nelson. Settings include blue diamond turquoise in the bola at left, blue gem turquoise in the other bola, and pink ice in the bracelet. The earrings and necklace are set with coral, the pendant with rutiled quartz.

myself. I saw prehistoric pieces and just had to try it. I attended IAIA during the 'golden era.' All 'the guys' [now well-known Indian artists] were there. We had the run of the place. We did whatever type of art we wanted, whenever we felt like it. I was amazed just reading about all these other potters who were doing exactly the same thing; I had to be different. I built my pottery thin from the very beginning." Using micaceous clay from the Taos area, Christine creates beautiful plainwares with sculptural shapes or adds an occasional appliquéd design. The beauty of much contemporary Navajo pottery comes from its symmetry and the natural "fire clouds" acquired during the firing process.

No other Navajo art style has evolved to jewelry's high level, but Fidel Bahe still laughs about his first try at silversmithing. "I'd seen lots of people make jewelry and decided I could, too," he said. "I bought a few tools, a torch, a bottle of acetylene, and some silver, thinking I'd make a buckle. I ended up with an empty

Fourteen-karat gold and coral jewelry by Harvey Begay, whose contemporary designs are unparalleled. The feather pattern was inspired by an ancient Mimbres black-on-white pottery design.

acetylene bottle and a blob of silver." Needless to say, Fidel has overcome that problem.

Contemporary jewelry artists are extraordinary craftsmen whose designs are superbly unique. This genre of jewelers includes some of the very best. Both silver and gold are set with turquoise, various colors of coral, lapis lazuli, shell, jet, opals, diamonds, and other precious and semi-precious stones.

"I bought a few tools, a torch, a bottle of acetylene, and some silver, thinking I'd make a buckle. I ended up with an empty acetylene bottle and a blob of silver."—FIDEL BAHE

Turquoise remains one of the most popular, but due to a shortage of the American stones, the use of Chinese turquoise is becoming more commonplace. Gene Waddell, of Waddell Trading Company in Tempe, Arizona, says that "like American turquoise, the Chinese stone is procured from several different mines and its quality ranges from poor to excellent. However," he added, "most Indian artists insist on using only the best." The best equals the finest grades of American stones in both quality and beauty.

Although early Navajo smiths were not noted for their lapidary skills, today's contemporary jewelers do excellent work. Not only are they expert at setting stones, but excel at channel work and mosaic inlay, techniques more common among the Zuni.

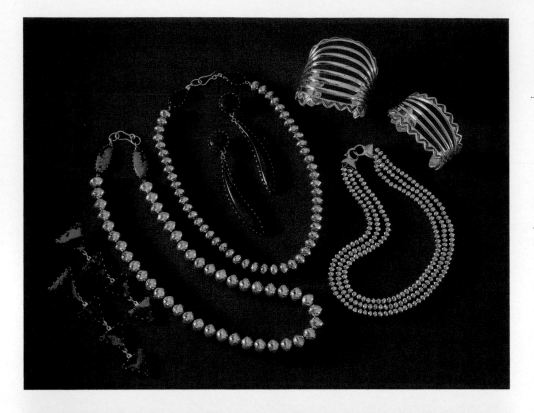

TOP LEFT: *The simple but beautiful silver styling of Deborah Silversmith. Her bracelets are remniscent of those made by her grandfather, Kenneth Begay, who taught her to do silverwork. The earrings are set with Royston turquoise, the necklace with lapis lazuli and Hachita turquoise from New Mexico.*

BOTTOM LEFT: *Richard Tsosie is noted for jewelry styles that combine overlay with heavily textured (granulated) surfaces. These unique pieces include malachite, lapis lazuli, red and pink coral, mother-of-pearl, onyx, and ironwood. The Spiderweb turquoise in the buckle and the side of the bracelet is Nevada blue; the remaining turquoise is Sleeping Beauty.*

OPPOSITE: *The artistry of Herbert Taylor. This photograph shows the stages of making the silver overlay necklace at top right, including the initial design. The overlay process involves meticulously cutting designs from silver, then soldering them to a silver backing. The black background is achieved by oxidation. Each link of the necklace is hinged to insure that it fits properly. Small pieces of coral were cut and polished to fit in channels around the edges of the necklace, and the pendant is set with Number Eight Spiderweb turquoise. Although the technique is not used in this necklace, silver filings as seen here are often sprinkled onto a silver surface and fused with a torch, which results in a textured finish. This technique, referred to as granulation or fused metal, may be seen in the textured surfaces of Richard Tsosie's jewelry at bottom left.*

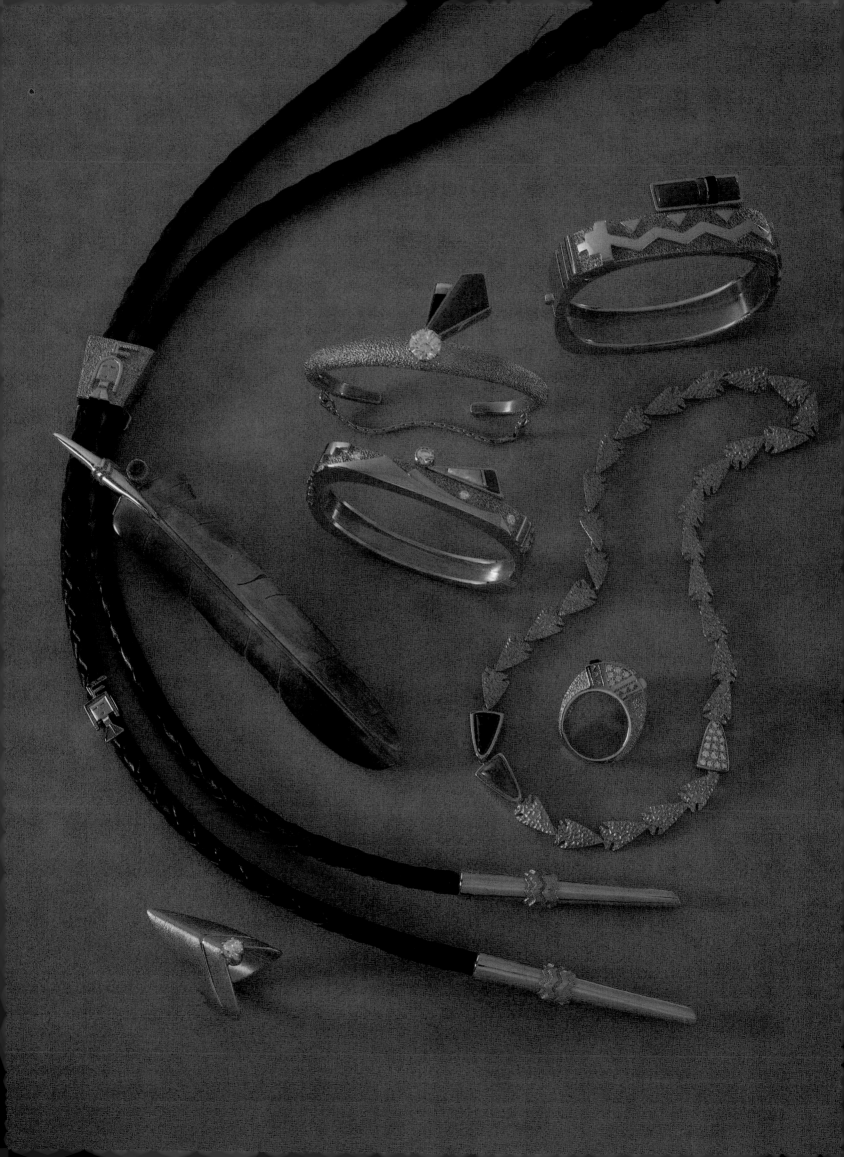

Many different techniques are employed by jewelry artists, and most combine several to achieve their artistic goals: tufacast, fabrication, and lost-wax cast, plus decorative techniques such as stamping, filing, repousse, appliqué, granulation, reticulation, engraving, and a technique that was once almost exclusive to the Hopi—overlay.

Contemporary Navajo jewelery styles began with the late Kenneth Begay, an innovative jeweler who carved a niche for himself in Navajo art history with his jewelry. He also taught or influenced many others, most prominently his son Harvey, who has gone on to become one of the top contemporary jewelers whose work is both stunning and unique. "My legacy from my father was 'Do something new,' " Harvey said. "As I got into jewelry more and more, I realized that the possibilities are endless—there's more than I could do in a lifetime. I constantly change things so if people try to copy my work I'll still be ahead of them. My job is to explore new ideas and new ways to work the metal. Everything I do is speculative because I reach out where others don't go."

Kenneth Begay also taught his granddaughter Debbie Silversmith to create beautiful jewelry, and she employs the same simple flair for which his work was noted. "He was the originator of the style," Debbie said, "but I added a few of my own ideas, like my stamp work around the edge. I started making beads for him when I was only twelve. I still love beads. He told me that Navajos wear necklaces because they represent life—the umbilical cord. I guess that's why I like to make them so much."

James Little, another leader among contemporary gold- and silversmiths, transforms childhood memories into classic jewelry art. "I just see things," James said. "I grew up in a hogan on the reservation. I know the old way. I hear it, I see

LEFT: Buffalo *is a bronze sculpture cast from a soapstone original carved by Fred Begay. This contemporary piece is 15" tall and 18 1/2" long.*

BELOW: Whale Watcher, *an Italian marble sculpture by Albert Jim, is 12 1/2" tall and 14" wide.*

it, I smell it. When I work, I turn that around and put the old ideas into new ways. But I want each piece to be special, to mean something. I don't like to just design 'something pretty.' Sometimes it takes a long time. I bought a piece of [fossilized] ivory at a gem show just because I liked the color. About a year later,

"I grew up in a hogan on the reservation. I know the old way. I hear it, I see it, I smell it. When I work, I turn that around and put the old ideas into new ways."—JAMES LITTLE

BELOW: *A 48" by 73" Teec Nos Pos rug by Evelyn Poyer. Teec Nos Pos rugs are woven in a variety of color combinations, and are noted for their size and complexity. Surrounded by a wide border, the inner area is very elaborate and "busy" with diagonal lines, stylized arrows and feathers, diamonds, triangles, zigzags, angular hooks, lightning paths, and other geometric designs.*

I cut a piece off, which left a slice of it. I had it for seven or eight years, and every once in a while, I would pick it up and hold it. I would look at it and feel it, but couldn't decide how I wanted to use it, so I would put it away. One day I saw it lying there and it suddenly looked like an eagle feather. I just started cutting it down. I didn't want to rush. At first I thought it might be a pendant, but it was too long. Then I thought of the eagle and how the medicine men use eagle feathers to pray and how important the eagle is to all Indians, so the idea came to me to make a bola tie. You just have to wait sometimes and let it happen. It's interesting to see what comes out."

It is indeed interesting "to see what comes out" of James' creative mind through his talented hands. Especially when one realizes that his chances of succeeding in the contemporary art world were very slim. Due to a hearing impairment, most of James' early years were spent herding sheep instead of attending school. At eighteen, he had little education and spoke no English but, with his hearing restored through a series of surgeries, he set out to learn the basics of silversmithing at Navajo Community College. After studying there under Kenneth

148   EVENING - TWILIGHT

Begay, James set out on his own. Launched into a strange, and often hostile, new world, he not only learned to speak English but, through private tutoring, to read and write the language. As his skills improved and his world expanded, so did his ideas and creativity. Through some form of metamorphosis, he is able to transform his memories into exquisite contemporary stylings of gold and silver set with diamonds, turquoise, coral, and other stones.

"This makes up both worlds—the old world (the traditional way) and the new world. Life is represented by the beauty of the piece."—RICHARD TSOSIE

Richard Tsosie learned jewelry-making from his brother Boyd, who also studied under Kenneth Begay. In their youth, they lived at Wide Ruins, and Richard says, "There's a lot we did without, like running water and electricity, but we didn't miss the things we'd never had. We had much more. My memories of my childhood are very pleasant. When we came to town, it was a whole different world, so we learned to deal with both worlds as one. Certain symbols in my jewelry are used to remind me of that. The lightning represents the natural environment; the arrow represents things made by hand. This makes up both worlds—the old world (the traditional way) and the new world. Life is represented by the beauty of the piece."

As artists strive to surpass their own previous works, as well as those of others, the same words are heard time and again: "I wanted to do something different." That is exactly what contemporary artists are doing, yet they continue to include the beauty and harmony so necessary to the *Diné*.

AS TWILIGHT DEEPENS INTO DARKNESS, Navajo artists prepare to march boldly into the twenty-first century.

BELOW: A Drink from the Wash, *a 10" by 20" watercolor by Calvin Toddy.*

OPPOSITE: The Elusive Cup, *a 40" by 30" watercolor by Teddy Draper Jr., won Second Prize at the 1993 Gallup Intertribal Indian Ceremonial.*

NIGHT-DARKNESS

In a Holy place with a God I walk

In a Holy Place with a God I walk

On a chief of a mountain with a God I walk

In old age wandering with a God I walk

On a trail of Beauty with a God I walk

— Mountain Song, from The Nightway

ABOVE: Grandpa Stones, *an 18" by 24" oil on canvas by Marvin Toddy.*

PREVIOUS PAGE: Knights of Fire, *a 24" by 18" colored pencil by Wayne Beyale, won First Prize at the 1993 Santa Fe Indian Market.*

NIGHT-DARKNESS

Millions of stars twinkle in the black night. A slight breeze teases the treetops and only

the rustle of rodents and small animals disturbs the silence. The eastern sky begins

to glow; the moon peeks over the mountain. The moonlit valley floor

is bright against the deep shadows of cliffs and trees.

The misty glow that hovers wraithlike among the shadows gives rise to ancient legends as the canyon echoes back the call of the coyote.

Yei'ii bichai dancers perform in front of a ceremonial hogan; a bonfire blazes nearby and the aroma of juniper smoke hangs in the air. The People who have gathered for the ceremony move quietly in the flickering firelight, each breath puffing out like smoke in the frigid air. Packed snow crunches underfoot, and the soft murmur of voices gently ripples through the crowd like leaves drifting with the breeze. It is almost midnight on a cold winter's night, the time for healing ceremonies; a time when the power of the Holy People becomes a living force.

In the walk along the Beauty trail, it is also winter, and the end of life draws near. Night-Darkness is a time for reflection—of remembering the old ways and strengthening traditions. It is a time that brings families together; stories are told of the past and ancient legends are recounted.

It is these stories and legends that often kindle the fires of imagination in today's artists. It is this family time that they often recall with fond memories: herding sheep, the landscape, the hogan, weavers, the family and, most notably, grandparents. Although artists often mention their parents with affection and pride, it is the grandparents who are revered. They are the ones who are quoted and are spoken of time and again: "I lived with my grandparents"; "I stayed with my grandparents in the

This 48" by 36" oil on canvas by Clifford Beck won Best of Division at the 1992 Santa Fe Indian Market. The title, Twilight, refers to both the age of the couple portrayed in the painting and the fading light that illuminates their faces. "I prefer to paint the older people," Clifford says, "the more traditional ones who have retained our culture and have persevered in spite of the influences and pressures from the modern world around them. They have a lot of pride. That is what I wanted to capture."

summer"; "My grandmother taught me to weave"; "I learned to identify different plants and herbs from my grandmother"; "She told me about the Holy People as we herded sheep"; "She taught me the place of women in Navajo society"; "My grandfather taught me to do silverwork"; "He taught me how to build a hogan"; "He told me the stories of our clan." It goes on and on.

Painter Redwing Nez, who lives in Tuba City, Arizona, built a studio near his grandmother's home at Indian Wells, Arizona, where he lived as a youngster, and spends as much time as possible working there. "I want to hang onto that velvet shirt just a little while longer," he said with poignancy.

Because of the emotional ties to grandparents, art that features the elderly is also poignant, yet exhibits the strength and dignity of the People.

Clifford Beck says that his paintings are "paying homage to a way of life, especially my paintings of the older folks. I see their pride and strength. They're watching their own way of life change. They're sort of the last of a kind, and this is very important to me."

Mark Silversmith remembers "walking through the snow from my parents' to my grandparents' hogan, and enjoying the peace and quiet that the snow brings. I guess that's why I tend to paint snow scenes now. People often comment on how peaceful my paintings appear. My grandparents were traditionalists. We helped chop wood, haul water, and herd the sheep to the high-country camp in summer. My grandfather told us the stories, and it made the old days seem real."

"I want to hang onto that velvet shirt just a little while longer."——REDWING NEZ

Jewelry by Boyd Tsosie. The necklace is coral, and the earrings are set with high-grade Tibetan turquoise. The ring is embellished with the intricate sculpted flower-and-leaf design for which Boyd is noted.

Grandparents often cared for the children, nurturing them throughout their childhood. They were the ones who usually taught the children the ways of nature and about the Navajo Way, who told and retold the stories and legends while herding sheep or sitting around the fire at night. It is surely no accident that two of the most prominent deities of the Navajo, Changing Woman and Talking God, are referred to as the Grandmother and Grandfather of the People.

"Although I live in an urban area," Vernon Begaye said, "I go back to my grandparents' and see them living the way people talk about. They still live the old way, and it makes it all seem very real."

"I grew up on my grandparents' ranch," David Draper says. "I began drawing animals, especially horses, which signify strength, beauty, and free spirit. Animals were my first models and, with my grandparents' encouragement, my goal to be an artist was set."

Naveek learned the rudiments of silverwork from his Navajo grandfather, a *hataałi* who often took the boy along on his travels to see patients. "When we visited Chaco Canyon," Naveek said, "my grandfather would say: 'Listen, listen. Listen to the spirits. There were once children like you who lived here—who played here. Now they are gone, but their spirits still live. Listen to the spirits. Never forget them.'" Naveek and his grandfather returned often to Chaco, both during the day and at night, and Naveek remembered.

LEFT: *Don Clark's 30" by 22" pastel,* Friends in the Dark, *is one of his "blanket series." "Darkness plays a powerful role in the lives of most people," Don said. "It is something that most everyone can relate to in some way. I often use a black background to represent the power and uncertainty which darkness brings. We seek comfort, warmth, security, and protection, which is symbolized by the blanket in my work."*

BELOW: In Grandma's Care, *a 26" by 18" pastel by Johnson J. Yazzi.*

When requested to make a piece "that comes from your heart," Naveek created a necklace entitled *Children of Chaco* that won numerous awards. Other exquisite pieces of jewelry often reflect his memories of that night sky.

Baje Whitethorne's memory is one that carries over into the surrealistic skies of his paintings. "One day we were out herding sheep," Baje explained. "On the way home for lunch, the sky suddenly turned dark. My grandfather said the Sun had died and we must wait for it to be reborn. I wanted to eat and drink, maybe take a nap, but he said we must do nothing until it was reborn. Later, he told me about an eclipse and drew a big red sun. I was fascinated. I painted that sun everywhere—on cardboard boxes, on the hogan, on the stove, even on the side of the pickup and, of course, I got in big trouble. But that story's going to come out now in a children's book I'm working on."

"When I grow old, I want to know I've left something behind. Not as an artist, but as a human being who loves and cares and tends and helps others. To do that is to Walk in Beauty."—MARY MOREZ

This unusual pottery jar is 17" tall and 12 3/4" in diameter. Made by Lorraine Williams, it won First Prize, Best of Category, and Best of Division at the 1993 Museum of Northern Arizona Navajo Artists Exhibition. Just above the yei'ii figure is an "opening" in the design. This assures that the potter's ideas and designs are not closed within.

Jesse Monongye, who creates magnificent inlaid bear pendants, told this story of his grandfather. "The bear is a symbol of strength and power. Once my grandfather and I came across a bear in the mountains. A *bi-i-i-g* guy. Grandfather spoke to the bear in Navajo, acknowledging his strength and power, asking for blessing and to pass safely. The bear got down and walked away into the woods. That really made an impression on me.

"My grandmother taught me respect for the environment," Jesse added, "and the old Navajo way of discipline and about the Beautyway. She said that all Creation begins at the center from within. If you look at the center of a loom, the colors of a new design will show themselves to you and each design will come only once. She said that the yellow poles that hold up a loom must be strong or the loom will sag and the rug will be crooked. A human has to live between the yellow poles of his life, too—not too poor, not too rich—to stay in harmony."

Redwing Nez's late grandfather really knew how to keep a young fellow in line. He was not unduly impressed by Redwing's success. "It didn't matter how well I'd done," Redwing said with a grin. "I'd come home telling him stories of my travels and meeting famous people, but my grandfather always just shook his head and said: 'It don't matter where you go or what you do, you're always gonna come home and eat these sheeps.' "

"Old people are to be revered," Mary Morez said, "for their wisdom, their experience, and their ongoing teachings. . . . When I grow old, I want to know I've left something behind. Not as an artist, but as a human being who loves and cares and tends and helps others. To do that is to Walk in Beauty. Besides, I feel that my greatest achievement is my daughter Sheila and my new grandchild."

Wisdom is held in high regard in Navajo society and wisdom comes with maturity; therefore, the teachings and experiences of the elders are very important. The *hataałis,* who are the most respected of men, study for many years to learn the intricacies of their practice, earning that respect.

ABOVE: *Gold and silver overlay jewelry by Kee Nez.*

OPPOSITE: *This double-exposure photograph shows the front and back of a sculpture by Harold Davidson that is 15 1/2" tall and 18" wide. Inspired by a trek into the San Francisco Peaks, the Sacred Mountain to the West, Harold carved* Song of the Mountain. *It represents the Four Sacred Mountains and* yei'iis *during a ceremony. The lightning symbol on Talking God (center) signifies the belief that* yei'iis *must not be talked about after the first lightning strikes in spring.*

Ritual is a necessity in maintaining balance and harmony. Not only are lengthy and complex ceremonies involved, but prayers are offered for specific blessings. "I still tend to go to Talking God with my problems," Redwing Nez says. "I've fallen into the pattern of talking to him."

Harold Davidson says that "whichever god someone believes in must be right for him. I feel that God gave me the talent to make beautiful things. I pray in my shop and talk to the stones; my art is very spiritual. Everyday, I thank God for what he's done for me and for others who are trying. Whatever happens in my life and to my art, it's all up to God."

"God has honored me with a gift," Charles Morris said, "and I thank him for it. A lot of good artists are thankful for their talent, but they don't acknowledge where it comes from. I thank God for this gift."

"Looking back," Vernon Haskie said, "I'm amazed at how far I've come. A lot of people are craftsmen; only a few have the creativity to be artists. I'm thankful for all that's happened and for the prayers of my father."

Many artists depend on prayer to maintain harmony, and jewelry, paintings, sculpture, and other arts find their way to a *hataałi* for prayer before being presented to the public.

"I try to take my jewelry to my dad for him to pray over it before a show," Herbert Taylor said. "I didn't do it this year, and I only won one ribbon. I have to get back to doing things right."

His brother Robert also depends on his father's prayers to "get things right." Plagued by a hand that would no longer work properly, Robert went to his father. "He used 'hand trembling' to find my problem," Robert explained. "He said someone who owned a piece of my jewelry had died and been buried with it on. That meant a part of me had been buried, too." The prayers of a healing ritual cured Robert's hand and he has worked with no difficulty since.

"I pray in my shop and talk to the stones; my art is very spiritual. . . . Whatever happens in my life and to my art, it's all up to God."—HAROLD DAVIDSON

Although Myra Tso has a degree from Northern Arizona University, Flagstaff, in ceramics, she clings to the old ways of making pottery. "I could use new techniques," Myra said, "but our old ways almost died out and I want to keep using them. I recently did this series of pots that were more like effigies or fetishes instead of just ornamental figures. My grandfather was a *hataałi,* and he

ABOVE: Night Chant, a 9 1/2" by 35" sand-painting by Joe Ben Jr. Although many artists recreate traditional sandpainting designs, Joe's incomparable work goes far beyond. He uses sandstone with more exotic materials such as gold, lapis lazuli, sugilite, turquoise, azurite, coal shale, gypsum, sandstone, sulfuric material, hematite, and diamond dust to create legendary figures in ceremonial scenes. Here, yei'iis from the Nightway cere-mony rise over the four Sacred Mountains into a night sky filled with sparkling dia-mond-dust stars.

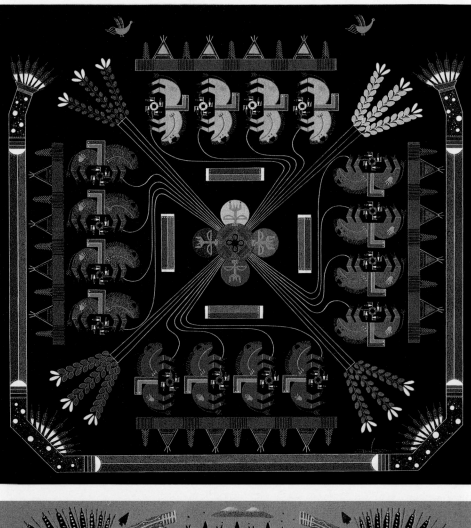

THIS PAGE AND OPPOSITE, BOTTOM:
Artists often recreate traditional sandpaint-
ings from Navajo ceremonies; however,
designs are altered to avoid sacrilege. Here,
three artists offer their interpretations of a
sandpainting from the Shootingway. The
sandpaintings on this page, both titled
Home of the Buffalo, *portray designs that*
represent the Buffalo People and the tepees
that are their homes. The white lines are the
trails to water, and the four sacred plants
grow from the center toward each corner. The
25 1/2" by 25 1/2" contemporary work of Joe
Ben Jr. (above right) includes sandstone, gold
dust, and finely ground lapis lazuli, azurite,
hematite, and coal shale. In her 16" square
sandpainting (below right), Diane Thomas
used more traditional materials: sands ground
from stones gathered from various New
Mexico locations. Alberta Thomas wove a
similar sandpainting design into her 66" by
62" rug, The Buffalo Who Never Die,
opposite.

was so special to me. In the fall, he would slip up to me very quietly and whisper that we should go. We would go up on the mountain where he would sing and say a prayer for me. It was just between us. My grandfather still sings in the Four Winds. His prayers for his granddaughter are for all time. My grandfather is gone, but I can still hear his songs in the wind. I hope anyone who buys a piece of my pottery will hear and care more about the story behind it than just the shape of the pot. The older ones in my family are beginning to die out now; that's why I want to stick to traditional pottery.

"There is a certain ritual—you put the horned toad on your heart and say a prayer. That horned toad carries your prayers for a year."—MYRA TSO

"The horned toads on my pottery are also very special. When we were kids, we'd go out in the spring and find a horned toad. There is a certain ritual—you put the horned toad on your heart and say a prayer. That horned toad carries your prayers for a year. Some of them have a yellow streak down their back.

Those you don't bother. They are already carrying some other child's prayer."

All ritual and ceremonies are essential parts of the Navajo Way, and sandpainting art is inspired by those that are created ceremonially. Joe Ben Jr., who began taking part in ceremonial sandpaintings when he was only eight, is today the master of this specialized contemporary art. Taking advantage of nature's palette, he uses "dust" from gold, diamonds, lapis lazuli, turquoise, and other semi-precious stones in his "paintings." "When sandpaintings are done ritually," Joe explained, "other elements are also used—corn meal, charcoal, water, corn pollen—natural materials from other areas. As my world became larger, I saw my inner world broadening; as my travels increased, so did my ideas. I began to interpret myself differently, and gradually began working with other materials." Like other artists, Joe alters colors and

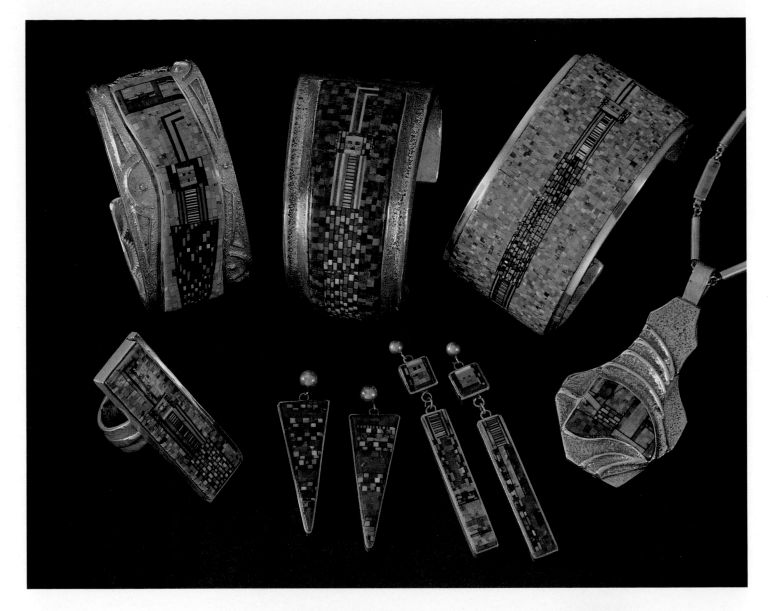

ABOVE: *Carl and Irene Clark use a micro-fine inlay technique patterned after that of European master jewelers of the eighteenth and nineteenth centuries. Irene does most of the design and metalwork; Carl does the lapidary. Stones include lavulite (purple), lapis lazuli, jet, turquoise, red and pink coral, and white shell. The prevelant motif is the Rainbow Yei'ii, a symbol of protection.*

RIGHT AND OPPOSITE: *Faye Tso's canteen appliquéd with a yei'ii design (right) won Second Prize at the 1993 Museum of Northen Arizona Navajo Artists Exhibition. It is 8 3/4" tall and 8" wide at the handles. The large pieces of pottery pictured opposite were made by Myra Tso, Faye's daughter. The vase with appliquéd yei'iis and the human figure are 28" and 22 1/2" tall respectively; the water jar with horned toads is 15" long. The clay sculpture,* For All Time, *was made to honor her grandfather, who sang and prayed for her. "He was very special," Myra said. "My grandfather sings in the Four Winds. His prayers are for his granddaughter for all time. Grandfather is gone now, but I can still hear his songs in the wind."*

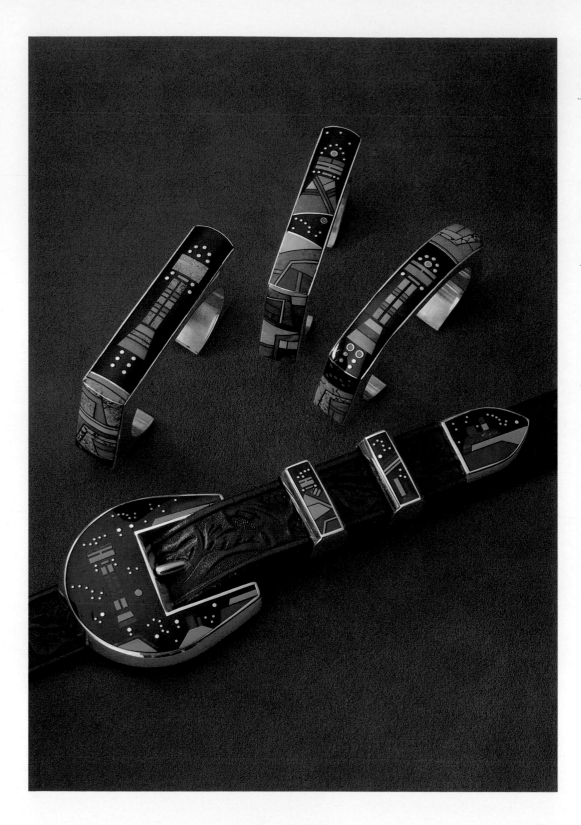

LEFT AND OPPOSITE: *Jimmie Harrison portrays yei'ii figures in his finely executed inlay work (left), which incorporates turquoise, jet, Mediterranean red coral, China pink coral (from the South Seas), sodalite (light purple), lapis lazuli, variscite (green), and mother-of-pearl. Al Nez used a similar motif in his gold jewelry (opposite) set with turquoise, red and pink coral, lapis lazuli, and opal. All of the pieces are tufacast except the center necklace. "I like the contrast of textures," Al said. "I enjoy playing with tufastone, carving it and experimenting. Tufa is challenging. It has to be perfect. It's like sculpting a design in reverse."*

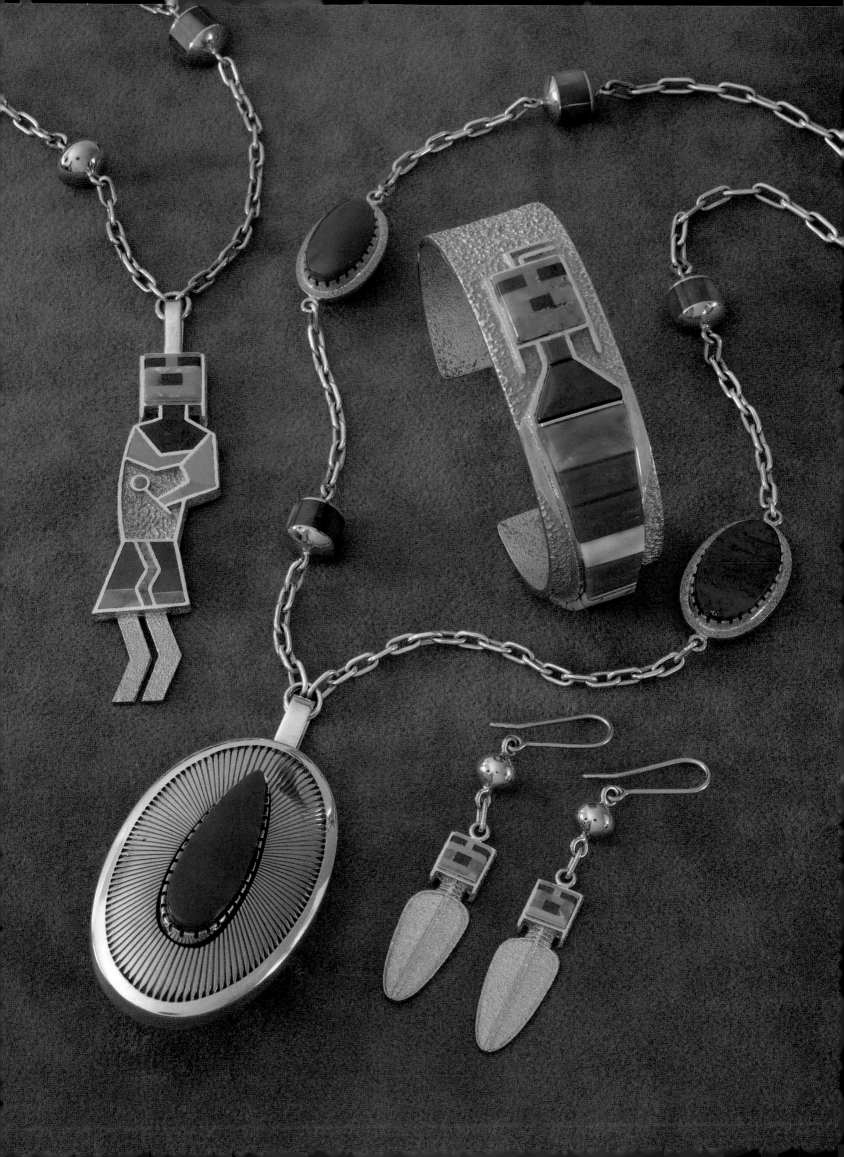

Spirit Canyon, *a 9" by 22" etching by*
Wallace N. Begay, won First Prize in
Original Graphics at the 1993 Museum of
Northern Arizona's Navajo Artists
Exhibition.

designs when portraying the Holy People and other sacred images. He not only does sandpainting designs, but Navajo scenes such as the Nightway in which the *yei'iis* rise above the sacred mountains into a star-filled sky.

The importance of the Holy People is apparent by their prominence in Navajo art. Carl and Irene Clark use the Rainbow *Yei'ii* extensively in their jewelry designs. "That figure is the one medicine men begin their sandpaintings with during a healing ceremony," Carl explained. "The Rainbow *Yei'ii* is a symbol of protection."

Jewelry, sculpture, weaving, pottery, sandpaintings, baskets, and paintings all include artists' interpretations of the *yei'ii* as well as other sacred symbols. However, order is very important to the Navajo, so it is imperative that they be used only in the proper manner.

Basketmaker Lorraine Black says that she "can't weave just anything. Before weaving a bear or coyote, I have to ask permission of the elders. If I weave a crooked Rainbow *yei'ii,* then I'll be bent. *Yei'iis* are perfect, and they must be done right."

"I want my interpretation of these deities to . . . support a system of belief which I feel is the most important part of Indian existence."—TONY ABEYTA

Herbert Taylor uses traditional designs in his jewelry, but if they are sacred, they are not replicated exactly. He received the consent of his father before using the designs. "My dad said, 'It's all right. Who would understand? Only if you already know, would you understand what they mean. The Holy People are too strong to be bothered by this.'"

Bob Lansing will not carve bears in his pottery designs without first going through a ceremony that purifies him and permits him to do so. "The bear is the Brother to the Navajo," he explained. "He protected them on their journeys through the other worlds. He is greatly revered. I also don't put sandpainting designs on my pottery," he added. "If I did use them, the pots couldn't be fired because sandpaintings can't be burned."

Tony Abeyta offered his thoughts on painting the sacred *yei'ii*. "Because of the nature of these images and the restrictions on portraying or painting them out of their sacred context, I choose to create my own interpretation—using nature and the ideas, healing, semblance, and unity of them as inspiration or motivation in the execution of each painting. I want my interpretation of these deities to support the ideas and beliefs instilled in them, and paint them to my fullest potential and, therefore, to support a system of belief which I feel is the most important part of Indian existence."

Clifford Beck adds that "as an artist, I find the *yei'iis* wonderful sources of inspiration. But as a Navajo, I can't view them simply as artistic subjects. Instead, it's necessary to approach the *yei'ii* not only with a view to artistic freedom, but respect as well. Somewhere in all of that lies a balance between reverence and artistic freedom."

This alabaster sculpture, The Gifts, *by Tomas Dougi Jr., won first prize at the 1985 Museum of Northern Arizona Navajo Artists Exhibition.*

Always there is mention of keeping that precarious balance in order to preserve harmony—balance between good and evil, between nature and man, between man and the deities. As artists struggle to maintain that delicate balance, they offer their own interpretation of sacred images.

These deities are also brought to life through oral tradition, as legends and stories of the past are told and retold. Night is the time for storytelling, and children sit spellbound by the fire, listening to Coyote stories or the legend of Changing Woman and her twin sons, Born for Water and Monster Slayer, who killed the monsters threatening to destroy the People. Storytellers are as important to the Navajo as medicine people. Through storytelling the elders not only recount past experiences, but teach the Creation story and the importance of their traditions.

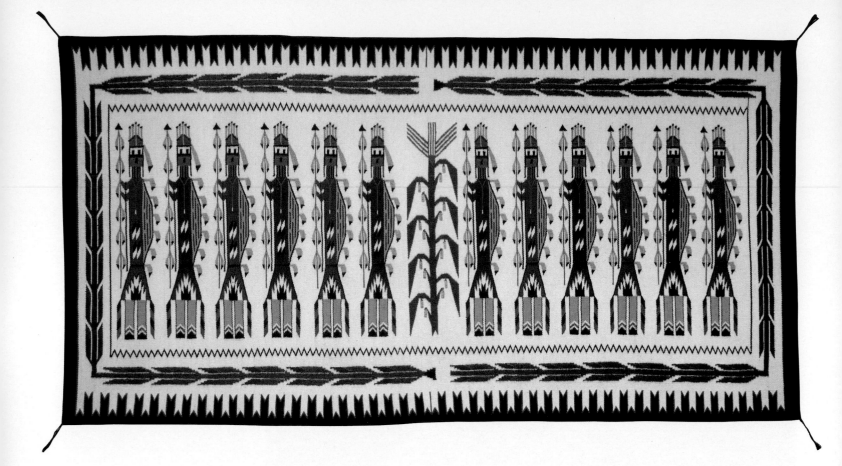

Mary Morez is dismayed by the fact that some Native Americans learn nothing of their culture. "I have a couple of Indian friends, a fashion model and an actor," she said, "who tell me they don't know what they are, that they don't understand what an Indian is, except that it is an empty space in their lives. They speak of their 'plastic and cement' world where people are cold, selfish, and use each other, a world in which the standard values are youth, money, drugs, sex, and the jet set. That doesn't mean they have to be plastic people themselves. How sad that they won't do a little study to learn their tribal philosophies and appreciate where they come from. They could be so comforted and could benefit by that knowledge."

"It's necessary to approach the yei'ii *not only with a view to artistic freedom, but respect as well. Somewhere in all of that lies a balance between reverence and artistic freedom."*

——CLIFFORD BECK

OPPOSITE, TOP: *Marilyn Paytianio wove this 38" by 71" pictorial that portrays the Humpback* Yei'ii. Yei'ii *rugs depict the Holy People in slender, stylized figures facing forward. Because of the sacredness of the figures, this rug is sometimes controversial, and weavers may have a ceremony performed to insure harmony.*

OPPOSITE, BOTTOM: *An unusual tapestry quality* yei'ii bichai *weaving by Della Woody. The top of this 39" by 65" rug includes pictorial figures; Navajo couples hold the smaller* yei'ii bichai *rug above as well as the large one below. Although* yei'ii bichai *actually means "Grandfather of the Deities," the word is commonly used to differentiate between the deities (*yei'iis*) and the human representatives who impersonate them during ceremonies. In* yei'ii bichai *rugs, the figures, who have human chacteristics, are shown in profile as though performing.*

The task of storytelling is an arduous one. The elder who tells the stories must sometimes prepare for a two- or three-night stint. Telling the Creation legend with its songs takes at least that long. Sometimes the children are given crafts to learn at this time. Winter darkness comes early, there is not much room to spare in a hogan and, since one rarely ventures out at night except to attend a ceremony, there can be a lot of hours to fill.

Elizabeth Abeyta remembers "all seven children in the family sitting around the table on stormy nights, working with clay or tie-dye or batiks."

Harvey Begay, who spent summer vacations with his grandparents, remembers the legends and stories. "My taste of reservation life was brief," Harvey said. "My grandparents didn't speak English; we herded sheep, came back home to eat, spent evenings with the uncles and aunts telling stories. The one I remember best, of course, was about *Yenaaldlooshii.* They tried to scare us into being good."

Yenaaldlooshii, or *maiitsoh,* the skinwalker, half man–half coyote or wolf, can run like the wind, even fly, and he comes out at night. He must be avoided at all costs—a very good reason to fear the dangers and evils that lurk during the hours of darkness. Skinwalkers and *tchindees* (ghosts), both of which are very real to the traditional Navajo, are rarely discussed. The People wish to avoid the mockery of non-Navajos, and they do not tempt fate by dwelling on the negative—say it, it might happen. Witchcraft can be controlled to some degree through ceremonies; witches can even be slain, but it is best to avoid them. One must always be on guard, and it is the night hours when one faces these evils.

Virgil Nez's painting *The Skinwalker* is very graphic. In fact, it is so graphic that Virgil has been criticized for his portrayal. "When I was a student at NAU, I wrote a paper in religion philosophy class on *Yenaaldlooshii,* the Skinwalker. I did a lot of reading about it and talked to my grandparents and others. I was taking an art class at the same time, and when I began painting him, I could feel the presence of powerful spirits. I was painting at night in a big room, all alone; outside, the pine trees were blowing in the wind. It was like opening doors to

ABOVE AND OPPOSITE: *Navajo artists tend to avoid such subjects as witches and ghosts due to the evil connected with these supernatural beings and the power they possess. But in 1959, Narciso P. Abeyta (Ha-so-deh) painted his interpretation of* The Werewolf, *a 29 1/2" by 19 3/4" tempera or watercolor on sandpaper (opposite). In 1992, Virgil J. Nez dared to tread on forbidden ground in portraying a powerful image of* yendalooshi *in his changing state.* Skinwalker *(above), a 48" by 72" oil on canvas, won First Prize and Best of Division at the 1992 Museum of Northern Arizona Navajo Artists Exhibition.*

another world. Navajos and other artists say I should not fool with it. It will kill you. I believe it, but I don't fear it. If you fear it, it can cause you harm. Maybe it's dangerous, but I want to see it. I respect it. I know it's out there.

"An important thing happened in 1983 when I encountered some 'force.' The dogs were barking outside. First 'it' came from the North, then the East, then the South. By the time it got to the West, I had a shotgun loaded and went out with my flashlight. I ran around the house and soon the dogs retreated toward me. They were really scared. Then the wind began to blow harder. I heard a noise like the cry of a baby from out there. It really began to sink in that this was something supernatural, but I wanted to know about it. If you fear it, it can take you over, but if you don't fear it, it's different. It lives off your fear and energy. It can hear your heartbeat. When you start fearing it, it takes over; you run, he's after you. You have someone trying to kill you. You have to be careful. I believe in it, but to say that is to open doors. Maybe I like to ride on the edge. We don't know how the spirits do it. But deep inside I want to have the power—not to turn into that, but to paint it. I have my own prayers and things to get the painting started."

"I was painting at night in a big room, all alone; outside, the pine trees were blowing in the wind. It was like opening doors to another world."—VIRGIL NEZ

The 16 1/2" diameter basket by Eleanor Rock shown at top features yei'iis and cornstalks symbolizing a prayer for rain and good crops; the 15" diameter basket by Jenny Rock (right) shows the Horned Monster in repeated designs separated by arrowheads representing protection against him; the 11 1/2" diameter basket by Peggy Rock Black (left) portrays the turkey of Navajo legend, the last creature to emerge into this world from the underworlds.

Virgil's dramatic painting, *The Skinwalker,* won Best of Division, Fine Arts in the 1992 Navajo Exhibition at the Museum of Northern Arizona. The following words are excerpts from a piece written by Bruce Hucko to accompany the exhibition of this painting: "Due to its subject matter, it [the painting] will encounter a variety of responses: from question to anger, confusion to wonder, denial to acceptance. . . . This artist put himself at risk, both personally and culturally, to create this piece. This was the only piece of art entered that said to me, 'I'm not quite sure what I'm getting into here, but I've got to do it. I am willing to explore unknown lands and use the skills I have to help bring this image forth.'. . . I doubt that this piece will coordinate with anyone's couch!"

While it is true that this is not a "comfortable" painting, it is a powerful piece that draws its strength from Navajo beliefs.

UNLESS ATTENDING A CEREMONY where they are protected by the power of the Holy People, the traditional *Diné* find warmth, security, and protection inside by the fire during the hours of darkness. The time not spent in sleep or story-telling are passed in conversation.

"A hogan is just a hogan until you put a song, a prayer, and a fire into it. Life isn't really life until you add a song and a prayer."—ROY WALTERS

White Shell Woman, *an Italian marble and steatite sculpture, 45" tall, is by Roy M. Walters Jr. The legendary White Shell Woman is sometimes synonymous with Changing Woman, and at other times is considered a separate individual.*

"Talking was our family unity," Redwing Nez said with a grin, "but we went to sleep as soon as it got dark. I was raised in a hogan; you get *real* close that way. You live right on top of each other; we almost knew what someone wanted before they asked for it. There was something safe about that round room, but it was just a hogan until my grandmother got sick when I was about nine. Then we cleared everything out and brought in fresh dirt; did all the things necessary for a ceremony, and the *hataałi* came. From then on, the hogan had new meaning for me. I realized that a hogan is like a mother, it provides you with everything. You can be born in a hogan, have a Blessingway, a *yei'ii* dance, squaw dance, get married, your children can be born there. A hogan is part of my brain—no corners, with a hole in the middle."

"A hogan is just a hogan," Roy Walters said, "until you put a song, a prayer, and a fire into it. Life isn't really life until you add a song and a prayer."

It is night, a time of darkness and uncertainty. But Night-Darkness is also a time of reflection and stories are told about the past—the history of the People, their perseverance and instinct for survival, the early days, and the old ways.

Baje Whitethorne remembers stories about Navajo rustlers. "My grandfather told us how the old Navajos used to steal cattle from the Spaniards, then hid out in remote canyons where they were never found. I remember those stories when I paint."

Books on Navajo history recount dozens of stories of this type, and a favorite is told by an old Navajo man in Ruth Underhill's 1956 book, *The Navajo:* "When they [the Mexicans] heard the cry 'Men of the Mountains,' every shepherd scurried for safety, leaving his flock unprotected. Two or three thousand sheep would be driven off at one time. But we always left a few ewes so the Mexicans could raise us another flock for next year."

Time spent on location for *Dances With Wolves* is responsible, at least in part, for Redwing Nez's decision to focus on one particular subject in his art. "I'm concentrating on just history for now," he said. "I want to tell some of my grandfather's stories in my paintings. I'm going into new areas with my art. When I was a kid, drawing was for my own amusement. This thing that I enjoyed was my friend. I was influenced early on by an artist I met as a kid when I was visiting my parents in L.A. I can't even remember his name, but he was a Venetian artist who painted seascapes. He was very quiet and neither of us spoke much English, but he gave me some watercolors and I learned a lot from him. At school, art became a competition. Ribbons are good for newcomers, I guess; the money is needed and it encourages artists.

ABOVE: Face of Prairie Scout, *a 23" by 30" mixed media by Redwing T. Nez, was inspired by the movie* Dances with Wolves, *in which he played the part of a Sioux warrior.*

RIGHT: *This 13" tall alabaster bust of a warrior and an eagle, a symbol of protection, was carved by Wilbert Kady. His work is signed with his grandfather's Navajo name, Kay-dih, which means the Last Born of the Family.*

Capturing Elk Medicine, *a 24" tall bronze sculpture by Oreland C. Joe Sr., was cast from a clay original. It depicts the celebration of a successful hunt by a Southern Ute hunter.*

The hoop in his left hand symbolizes the Circle of Life—eternity. Oreland's exceptional talent recently earned him a place among the Cowboy Artists of America, the first

Navajo—in fact, the first "thoroughbred" Native American—to become a member of that prestigious group.

Reminiscing, a 41 1/2" tall sculpture of Utah alabaster by Rickie Nez.

"But I'm tired of competing. I'm starting to venture out on my own, not thinking about what others are doing. A Navajo jeweler recently asked me how I handle business. I told him, I'm an artist; if business wants me, it will just have to find me. I think my art is different because I'm self-taught. I didn't study art; I just picked it up." He grinned and shook his head, then added. "But I was tricked, like Coyote. I thought I was going to go out and take the world by storm. Instead it's taken seventeen years of my life to get this far. But art wants me so badly; I'm doing everything I can. For now, I just want to do history."

Stories of the infamous Bosque Redondo days are told and retold in almost every family, and David Johns remembers them well. Braving an icy wind, we stood on a grass-covered hilltop as he pointed out his grandparents' hogan where he was raised, the places where he herded sheep, the sacred areas that were forbidden to him. "My grandfather was one of the ones who had to make 'The Long Walk,'" David said. "But he escaped and, although most of those who escaped either starved or were killed by Mexicans or people of other tribes, he made it home." David waved an arm into the distance. "My grandfather hid out in those canyons until the rest of the People returned."

David's memories of the past were put to the test in 1987 when he became a muralist, quite possibly the only Navajo to take on such a project. His "canvas" was the domed room at the top of a six-story building in Phoenix. Thirty-six feet in diameter with a dome rising fifty feet above the floor (a height comparable to an approximately four-story building), the area was finally transformed into an iconography of traditional designs, images from sacred legends, Native American historical figures, and landscapes. This dramatic blend of symbolism and realism, which took three years from planning stages to completion, was created by a master.

Some contemporary artists reach into the past for more than inspiration as they recreate old art styles. Several weavers replicate classic rugs of a style woven eighty to a hundred years ago, and Perry Shorty fashions a style of jewelry reminiscent of that made in the late 1930s and '40s.

"I just stuck with what I started out doing," Perry explained. "I make nearly all my own stamps. I bought them at first, but I didn't like them. They're for a different style, not mine. That's when I began making my own. I try to keep things simple; the old smiths didn't have a lot of tools and materials to work with." Perry adds that he often designs a piece without "knowing exactly how the finished piece will look." Perry may not know how the finished piece will look, but one can rest assured that it will be an extraordinary piece of jewelry. He is an excellent silversmith and his designs are exquisite.

The old becomes new; the new becomes old, and Navajo art continues its endless cycle. The People know that if all else fails, they can always depend on their art.

As Rosie Yellowhair said, "I've told my kids 'you'll never go hungry as long as you have your brushes and some paint.'"

Harold Davidson picks something up off the ground and stands looking at it. "I'm wondering what I can make out of it. There's always something there, you just have to think what you can do."

William Murphy won First Prize and Best of Category at the 1993 Gallup Intertribal Cermonial with Weary Warriors, *this 20" by 24" oil on canvas that depicts Navajo warriors after a skirmish with the cavalry.*

"Sometimes I go to sleep with a picture of a certain stone in mind," Herbert Taylor said. "When I wake up in the morning, I can still see it. And often I know what kind of jewelry I'm going to make for it."

Bob Lansing also dreams about his designs at times. "I've dreamed that I was showing a customer some of my work and I could even see the designs on it. I would scribble them out in the middle of the night, then try to figure it out the next morning."

"I've told my kids 'you'll never go hungry as long as you have your brushes and some paint.' "—ROSIE YELLOWHAIR

On the other hand, when James Little is doing a special piece, he says he can't sleep. "I'll be doing something, hear something, someone says something to me, and suddenly I see a picture in my mind. I have to get started on it."

Roy Walters made it sound very easy as he explained his first venture into sculpting. "I was a painter, but there was an awful lot of competition. My wife and I were driving through Utah one time and stopped at a rock shop. I saw a

ABOVE: Los Duenos del Mundo *(The Lords of the Earth) was an early 1800s term for the powerful Navajos who "ruled" the South-west. In this 48" by 60" oil painting of that title, Bill Dixon portrays Navajo warriors riding triumphantly through Monument Valley.*

RIGHT: After the Run, *a 48" by 44" oil on canvas by Andersen Kee. The artist says that this painting portrays no particular warrior, but is representative of one of Geronimo's men. Geronimo and his band gave the cavalry one last run before surrendering in 1886.*

ABOVE: Great Escape, *a 17" long and 8 3/4" tall wood sculpture by Henry W. Draper. This unusual figure carved from cottonwood root won First Prize at both the 1993 Museum of Northern Arizona Navajo Artists Exhibition and the 1993 Gallup Intertribal Indian Ceremonial.*

RIGHT: Heaven and Earth—The Change of Seasons, *a 44" by 42" acrylic and sand on canvas by Peter Ray James, was inspired by memories of his youth when he wandered among Anasazi ruins in his homeland near Pruitt, New Mexico. The artist says, "The Zuni Mountains, called the Dark Eyebrow Mountains by the Navajo, may be seen in the distance in the painting. It is October, the time when the yei'iis come out. The dark sky represents the changing seasons, the transition between fall and winter."*

piece of alabaster and bought it, took it home, and carved it. I thought it turned out pretty nice. It was a spontaneous thing. I knew the spark was there."

"Everything around us is made of Beauty that we can call our own and, in that manner, we link time and tradition into a chamber we will never forget."——PETER RAY JAMES

That spark is often ignited by memory. "My dad would tell the Creation stories," Beverly Blacksheep said. "They were stored in my memory. That piqued my interest and I've been painting traditional-contemporary ever since."

"Everything around us," Peter Ray James says, "is made of Beauty that we can call our own and, in that manner, we link time and tradition into a chamber we will never forget. My art is about tradition in transition."

Tim Washburn reflected on the early years. "My dad was a chanter and I remember him getting up early in the morning before sun-up to say prayers, but my folks died when I was eight and my sisters and I were taken from the reservation. I've moved my family back, but now we're in the computer age. My kids won't get the life I lived in the wagon days. My art comes from what I remember—from my heart. I try to get my feelings inside each piece."

Virgil Nez is another who was raised traditionally until he was fourteen. After the death of his father, he went to live with a family in Mesa, Arizona, and attend high school. "There was one thing that got me to leave the reservation," he laughed. "My brothers were always talking about a 'Big Mac.' That's what I wanted to see. That and a banana split." After earning a degree in illustration and painting at Northern Arizona University, Virgil and his family returned to

RIGHT: *The texture of Dawna D's sculptured pottery vessel gives it the appearance of leather; the miniature village tucked within its "canyons and cliffs" portrays a place once inhabited by the Anasazi.*

OPPOSITE: Broken Dreams, *Michael R. Sampson's 12" tall sculpture, depicts an ancient village tucked into a "cave" in what appears to be a broken Anasazi pottery jar. However, neither the vessel nor the village are formed from clay; this is a sculpture carved from soapstone.*

reservation life while awaiting acceptance to begin work on his master's degree. "It's really strange," Virgil said with a grin. "We've been living out on the reservation. I've just been painting, and it's so peaceful and quiet. I got into the Registrar's Office at ASU and felt like an alien. After all that time I spent attending the university, I suddenly felt like a sheepherder coming into the city for the first time."

"I grew up in Window Rock," Nelson Tsosie said. "We used to go around the back and climb all over it. It means a lot when I paint something like that now. Once I was away for about six months, and I got homesick. When I came back, I saw the reservation differently. It was like going back in time. When I started to realize that, I began wanting to preserve what I saw. I knew it was going to change."

"My art comes from what I remember—from my heart. I try to get my feelings inside each piece."—TIM WASHBURN

Reservation life has changed and will continue to do so. Where once the Navajo fought to keep their children from forced schooling, they now encourage them to get an education; where they once drove wagons, there are cars and pickups; where they once lived in hogans, there are now more modern homes; where they once eked out a livelihood from the land, many now find employment outside the Navajo community.

Still, the Navajo Way itself has not changed as drastically as some may think. Because their roots are so deeply embedded in the soil of the high plateau country, Navajo legends and history are written in the wind that blows across the

OPPOSITE AND BELOW: *Some weavers are replicating classic rugs from around the turn of the century. Shown opposite, Sarah Tsinnie wove this 63" by 38" replica of an 1890s child's wearing blanket. The 30" by 96" old-style Ganado runner below is by Pauline Yazzie. Although used occasionally as hall runners, these weavings are more commonly hung vertically in rooms with cathedral ceilings or diagonally along stairwells. Similar examples appeared in a catalog of Navajo weaving entitled* The Navajo, *which was published around 1911 by J. B. Moore, a trader at Crystal Trading Post.*

plains and in the canyons that cut into the depths of the earth. Their Place of Emergence is in a sacred area known as *Dinétah*. In that northeastern part of the reservation is Huerfano Mesa, the Sacred Mountain where Changing Woman was found; Shiprock and Grant's Lava Flow further south are where two of the monsters bent on destroying the First People were slain by the Hero Twins. The People have lived and farmed in Canyon de Chelly for generations, and White House Ruin is still home to the Holy People. It is there that Dawn Boy, Child of White Corn, crossed the canyon on a rainbow, singing as he entered the House of Dawn and Evening Twilight. He wandered in the House of Happiness, in the House of Long Life, with Beauty all around him and the pollen of Dawn upon his trail.

Spirituality is tied to these ancestral lands that lie between the Four Sacred Mountains, and many young people who live elsewhere return to the reservation for ceremonies or to request special prayers from *hataałis*. This demonstrates the strength of tradition, the one constant in a changing world. The art tradition is one that perhaps contributes the most to a flourishing culture.

"When I came back, I saw the reservation differently. It was like going back in time. When I started to realize that, I began wanting to preserve what I saw. I knew it was going to change."—NELSON TSOSIE

Walking along the Trail of Beauty is a way of life for Navajo artists, just as creating beauty and harmony are. When Navajo weavers tear down their looms and silversmiths put away their tools, when painters stack up their easels and sculptors lay aside their chisels, when potters toss out their clay and basketmakers

no longer gather sumac, when sandpainters discard their array of colored sands, then there will be no more Navajo Way.

"All I ask when I paint is daylight and a little peace and quiet. When I do hit a 'painter's block' I grab a saddle and go rope a horse . . . chase a cow around for awhile . . . I come back and hit it fresh. Then it's a blessing."——REDWING NEZ

What will happen to their culture in the future? What will become of their homeland? Just where will their art go from here? No one can know, but perhaps Redwing Nez's philosophy is best.

"All I ask when I paint is daylight and a little peace and quiet. When I do hit a 'painter's block,' I grab a saddle and go rope a horse. I ride to the trading post for a can of pop; cruise over the hills, ride down to the spring, across to where I

RIGHT: *This 48" square replica of an 1890s transitional style chief's blanket was woven by Sandy Nez. Navajo head men were never known as chiefs; the blankets were called this because of the prominent Plains and Pueblo people who traded for them. One of the earliest styles woven, these square rugs are characterized by plain designs in blue, red, white, and black. A chief's blanket is made so that when the four corners are folded to meet in the center, the design is the same as when unfolded.*

OPPOSITE: *Janet Tsinnie wove this 44" by 61" contemporary version of a historic "eye dazzler" rug at the request of trader Bruce Burnham. "I asked her to weave a Saltillo style," Bruce said, "which would have been woven in two sections and joined in the middle. Instead she used a Saltillo pattern with colors reminiscent of Germantown yarns to create an 'eye dazzler' effect. Looking at this rug is like looking down into a well."*

used to herd sheep. I go out and look for strays—chase a cow around for awhile. I come back and hit it fresh. Then it's a blessing. And wherever it's going to go, it's going to go."

IT IS NIGHT. The fire has burned low and all is quiet. Stars twinkle from on high and Darkness says: "Rest, my Grandchildren."

The world before me is restored in Beauty

The world before me is restored in Beauty

The world before me is restored in Beauty

The world before me is restored in Beauty

All things around me are restored in Beauty

It is finished in Beauty

It is finished in Beauty

It is finished in Beauty

It is finished in Beauty

—*from The Nightway*

GLOSSARY

Ahéhee—Thank you.

Bilagáanaa—Caucasian (Anglo).

Blessingway (Hózhǫ́ni)—The ritual first performed by the Holy People when they created man, the cornerstone of all Navajo ceremony. Insuring health, prosperity, and general well-being, the Blessingway is often held before embarking on any new undertaking.

Born for Water (To'Bájísh Chíní)—The younger of the Hero Twins born to Changing Woman.

Changing Woman (Asdzą́ą́ Nádłeehe)—The "Grandmother of the Navajos," Changing Woman is a prominant figure in the *Diné* creation story, mother of the Hero Twins—Monster Slayer and Born for Water—who rid the world of the monsters threatening to destroy the First People. Responsible for creating the first four clans, Changing Woman also established the Blessingway.

Dibé nitsaa—Mt. Hesperus in the La Plata Mountains of Colorado. Sacred Mountain to the North.

Diné—The People, the name preferred by the Navajos.

Dinétah—The Navajo "Holy Land" in northwestern New Mexico. This area includes the legendary Place of Emergence and is the ancestral homeland of the *Diné*.

Dook'o'oosłííd—The San Francisco Peaks of northern Arizona. Sacred Mountain to the West.

Gháá'ask'idii—The Humpback *Yei'ii*. The "hump" is actually a deerskin bag filled with seeds.

Hajiiníí—The Place of Emergence for the *Diné*.

Hand Trembler—A diagnostician; one who possesses a special gift of "seeing." In a trance-like state, he can reveal the location of missing persons or objects and, by passing a trembling hand over a patient, can diagnose the problem and recommend the proper healing ceremony.

Hataali—Medicine man, shaman, singer, chanter.

Hózhǫ́—The state of mind of the Navajo whose life is in total harmony; an ideal environment.

Hózhǫ́ náhastłíí—"It is finished in Beauty."

Iikááh—Sandpainting; literally, "the place where the deities come and go."

Jóhonaa'éí—The Sun.

Kiis'áánii—Pueblo group in Navajo legend.

The Long Walk—The more than three-hundred-mile forced trek to Bosque Redondo (Ft. Sumner, NM) that involved some 8,000 Navajos in 1863–64 after Kit Carson swept through Navajoland burning, razing, destroying everything in his path in order to defeat the *Diné*. After a four-year incarceration, the Navajos were allowed to return to their homeland, newly designated as a reservation. Even though they were faced with a barren land laid waste by Carson, they were glad to be home—back among the Four Sacred Mountains where their ceremonies would again be effective.

Monster Slayer (Naayéé' Neezghání)—The elder and dominant one of the Hero Twins.

Nightway or Night Chant (Tł'éé'jí)—A nine-day healing ceremony in which the *yei'ii bichai* partipate. It is often referred to as the *yei'ii bichai* ceremony.

Sháníidíín—A new beginning; literally, "the early morning sun's rays that streak upward through the clouds."
Sing—A chant or ceremony.
Sis naajini—Blanca Peak almost on the Colorado–New Mexico border. Sacred Mountain to the East.
Spider Woman (Na'ashjé'ii Asdzą́ą́)—One of the Holy People who assisted the Hero Twins and taught the Navajo to weave.
Squaw Dance (Nidáá')—A rite of the War Ceremony or Enemyway that somewhat resembles a girl's debut or "coming out" party. Young men must pay to dance with partners of their choice.

Talking God (Haashch'eelti'i)—A principal deity, leader of the *yei'iis;* known as the Grandfather of the Navajo.
Tchindii—Ghost.
Tsoodził—Mt. Taylor in northwestern New Mexico. Sacred Mountain to the South.

Yei'ii—The Holy People.
Yei'ii bichai—Literally, "the Grandfather of the Deities," but commonly used to mean the human representatives of the Holy People who take part in ceremonies.
Yenaaldooshii—The "Skinwalker," a most dangerous and malevolent spirit that appears at night and can change from human to animal form.

SUGGESTED READING

Adair, John. *Navajo and Pueblo Silversmiths.* Norman: University of Oklahoma Press, 1944. Reprinted 1989.

Beck, Peggy V. and Anna L. Walters. *The Sacred: Ways of Knowledge, Sources of Life.* Tsaile, Arizona: Navajo Community College Press, 1977.

Bedinger, Margery. *Indian Silver: Navajo and Pueblo Jewelers.* Albuquerque: University of New Mexico Press, 1973.

Evers, Larry, ed. *Between Sacred Mountains: Navajo Stories and Lessons from the Land,* vol. 2 of *American Indian Literary Series.* Tucson: University of Arizona Press, Suntracks, 1984.

Grant, Campbell. *Canyon de Chelly, Its People and Rock Art.* Tucson: University of Arizona Press, 1978.

Hartman, Russell B. and Jan Musial. *Navajo Pottery: Traditions and Innovations.* Flagstaff, Ariz.: Northland Publishing, 1987.

Hedlund, Anne Lane. *Beyond the Loom,* rev. ed. Boulder, Colo.: Johnson Books, 1990.

Kluckhohn, Clyde and Dorthea Leighton. *The Navajo.* Cambridge, Mass.: Harvard University Press, 1974.

Jacka, Lois Essary. *Beyond Tradition: Contemporary Indian Art and Its Evolution.* Flagstaff, Ariz.: Northland Publishing, 1988.

————. *David Johns: On the trail of Beauty.* Scottsdale, Ariz.: Snailspace Publishing, 1991.

Kaufman, Alice and Christopher Selser. *The Navajo Weaving Tradition: 1650 to present.* New York: E. P. Dutton, Inc., 1985.

Matthews, Washington. "Navajo Myths, Prayers, and Songs." *University of California Publications in American Archaeology and Ethnology,* vol. 5, no. 2 (1907).

Reichard, Gladys A. *Navajo Medicine Man Sandpaintings.* New York: Dover Publications, 1977.

Roessel, Robert A. Jr. *Dinétah, Navajo History,* vol. 2. Rough Rock, Arizona: Navajo Curriculum Center, 1971.

Underhill, Ruth M. *The Navajo.* Norman: University of Oklahoma Press, 1956.

Yazzie, Ethelou, ed. *Navajo History,* vol. 1. Rough Rock, Arizona: Navajo Curriculum Center, 1971.

Zolbrod, Paul G. *Dine bahane, The Navajo Creation Story.* Albuquerque: University of New Mexico Press, 1984.

ACKNOWLEDGMENTS

In mid-1993, we began working on a Navajo art book. Now thousands of miles, hundreds of sheets of film, and dozens of interviews later, here it is!

The time between has not been without incident—comical, inspirational, exhausting, emotional, stressful, wonderful. A lot of bleary looks passed between two weary people following the yellow line down some highway after attending yet one more Native American art exhibition. The "midnight oil" was burned both on the road and at home, as "shooting sessions" often lasted until two or three in the morning. At other times, the day began at that hour—ideas churned in my mind, and I rose to face the word processor.

However, despite the stress and strain, the sleepless nights, the monotony of travel, this was a very rewarding time—time spent with traders, gallery owners, museum staffs, art exhibition coordinators, private collectors, and most of all, the artists. We met some terrific Navajo people for the first time, visited with wonderful long-time Navajo friends. The confidence placed in us and our project was not only gratifying, but almost overwhelming. Without question, we were allowed to photograph art at museums and exhibitions. Traders, gallery owners, collectors, and artists either shipped art to us, brought it to us in person, or allowed us to take it to be photographed in the studio at our Phoenix home—all with no "strings attached" and no promises made.

To each and every one who so willingly offered assistance and encouragement, we can only say thank you. In addition to the artists who made their work available, art was furnished by the following:

Americana Indian Shows, Flagstaff, AZ
Arizona State Museum, University of Arizona, Tucson
Arroyo Trading Company, Farmington, NM
Artistic Gallery, Scottsdale, AZ
Bentley-Tomlinson Gallery, Scottsdale, AZ
James T. Bialac
Blair's Dinnebito Trading Post, Page, AZ
Blue Mountain Trading Post, Blanding, UT
Charles Azbell Gallery, Santa Fe, NM
Christopher's Enterprises, Albuquerque, NM
Cristof's Gallery, Santa Fe, NM
DeChelly Galleries, Chinle, AZ
Ellis Tanner Trading Company, Gallup, NM
Fifth Generation Trading Company, Farmington, NM
First American Traders, Gallup, NM

Four Winds Gallery, Pittsburgh, PA

Foutz Trading Company, Shiprock, NM

Gallery 10, Scottsdale, AZ

Gallup Intertribal Indian Ceremonial, NM

Garland's Indian Jewelry, Sedona, AZ

Garland's Navajo Rugs, Sedona, AZ

The Heard Museum Indian Fair and Market, Phoenix, AZ

The Heard Museum Shop, Phoenix, AZ

Hogan in the Hilton, Santa Fe, NM

Hubbell Trading Post, Ganado, AZ

Hugh Perry Gallery, Sedona, AZ

Michael Hughes

Indian Arts & Crafts Association, Albuquerque, NM

Jesse Monongye Studios, Scottsdale, AZ

La Fonda Indian Shop & Gallery, Santa Fe, NM

Lovena Ohl Gallery, Scottsdale, AZ

Many Hands Gallery, Sedona, AZ

Margaret Kilgore Collection, Scottsdale, AZ

McGee's Beyond Native Tradition Gallery, Holbrook, AZ

Moon Dancer, Redondo Beach, CA

Museum of Northern Arizona, Flagstaff, AZ

Museum of Northern Arizona Navajo Artists Exhibition, Flagstaff, AZ

Navajo Tea & Trading Company, Kirtland, NM

O'Odham Tash, Casa Grande, AZ

Palms Trading Company, Albuquerque, NM

Pierce Fine Art, Scottsdale, AZ

Pueblo Grande Museum Indian Market, Phoenix, AZ

R. B. Burnham Trading Company, Sanders, AZ

R. C. "Dick" Cline Land Company

Ray Tracey Galleries, Santa Fe, NM

Robert F. Nichols Gallery, Santa Fe, NM

Rocking Horse Ranch, Phoenix, AZ

Russell Foutz Indian Room, Scottsdale, AZ, and Farmington, NM

Sacred Mountain Trading Post, Flagstaff, AZ

Shiprock Trading Company, Shiprock, AZ

Silversmith Studio & Gallery, Farmington, NM

Southwest Collectibles, Palm Desert, CA

Southwest Trading Company, St. Charles, IL

SWAIA, Santa Fe Indian Market, Santa Fe, NM

Tanner-Chaney Galleries, Albuquerque, NM

Tanner's Indian Arts, Gallup, NM

Tobe Turpen Trading Company, Gallup, NM

Toh-atin Gallery, Durango, CO

Bob and Judy Trehearne

Troy's Western Heritage Gallery, Scottsdale, AZ

Tuba Trading Post, Tuba City, AZ

Turquoise Door, Tucson, AZ

Turquoise Tortoise, Sedona, AZ

Twin Rocks Trading Post, Bluff, UT

Waddell Trading Company, Tempe, AZ

Wadle Gallery, Santa Fe, NM

William L. White, M.D.

Thank you to Barton Wright, who wrote our introduction, and the others who went "above and beyond the call of duty" in numerous ways, including graciously sharing their knowledge and answering our many questions—no matter how often we called.

Bill Beaver	Mike Jacobs, University of Ariz.
James T. Bialac	Gina Laczko, The Heard Museum
Elijah Blair	Carol Leone, Museum of No. Ariz.
Jim Blair	Larry Linford
Kathy Blair	Martin Link
Bruce Burnham	Ron Lynn
Diane Dittemore, University of Ariz.	Bill Malone
Teddy Draper Jr.	Ann Marshall, The Heard Museum
William & Peggy Lanning Eiselor	Bruce McGee
Bill Faust	Mary Ann Mowry, Museum of No. Ariz.
Bill Foutz	Redwing T. Nez
Russell Foutz	Ken & Kathy Osborn
Michael J. Fox, Museum of No. Ariz.	Don Owen
Gwenn Gallenstein, Museum of No. Ariz.	Barry Simpson
Dan Garland	Steve Simpson
Al Grieve	Martin Sullivan, The Heard Museum
Ann Lane Hedlund, Ariz. State University	Joe Tanner
	Joe Tanner Jr.
Debra Hill, MNA	Carl Taylor
Byron Hunter	Herbert Taylor
Dina Huntinghorse	Jim Turpen
Robert W. Ingelholm Jr.	Eric Van Itallie
Peter Iverson, Ariz. State University	Gene Waddell
Martha Jackson, Navajo Community College	Edwin Wade, Museum of No. Ariz.
	Baje Whitethorne

To the *Diné* we must add a special word of thanks for their graciousness in sharing, not only their art, but their memories and philosophies, their hopes and dreams, their plans for the future.

INDEX

THE ART